Education for Purposeful Teaching Around the World

Purpose can be seen as a key promoter in both professional growth and resilience for teachers. As a result, in many countries around the world, the purpose of education and the role of schools as supports for purpose development are growing as important topics of scientific research and educational debate. A conceptual shift is occurring in several countries: the purpose of education is becoming an education for purpose. In this book, researchers around the world examine what a shift toward an education for purpose looks like across several cultures. Teachers around the world should be explicitly educated for competencies that make purposeful and purpose-oriented teaching possible. The goal of teacher education is to educate teachers not only to teach knowledge content, but also to reflect on the purposefulness of their teaching: Why do their lessons and activities matter? What immediate impact and long-term effects do their teaching efforts have on the pupils as well as the communities in which pupils interact?

The chapters in this book were originally published as a special issue of the *Journal of Education for Teaching*.

Kirsi Tirri is a Professor of Education and Research Director at the Helsinki Collegium for Advanced Studies at the University of Helsinki, Finland. She is also a Visiting Professor at St. John's University, USA and University of Tallinn, Estonia. Tirri has been the President of ECHA (European Council for High Ability) for the years 2008–2012, the President of the SIG International Studies at AERA (American Educational Research Association) for the years 2010–2013, and the President of the Finnish Academy of Science and Letters for the years 2016–2017.

Seana Moran is Research Assistant Professor of Developmental Psychology at Clark University, USA. Her research focuses on how individuals contribute to collaborations, society, culture, and other institutions, as well as how they come to recognize their actions as contributions to a greater good. More specifically, she writes about the intersections of life purpose, morality/ethics, creativity, culture, and wisdom.

Jenni Menon Mariano is Associate Professor of Education at the University of South Florida Sarasota-Manatee, USA. She teaches courses in child and adolescent development and learning, moral development and education, classroom assessment, and the psychology of life purpose. Her research examines positive human and community development in multinational contexts. She currently serves on the Executive Board of the Association for Moral Education and reviews for multiple research journals.

Education for Purposeful Teaching Around the World

Edited by
Kirsi Tirri, Seana Moran and Jenni Menon Mariano

LONDON AND NEW YORK

First published 2018
by Routledge
2 Park Square, Milton Park, Abingdon, Oxon, OX14 4RN, UK

and by Routledge
711 Third Avenue, New York, NY 10017, USA

Routledge is an imprint of the Taylor & Francis Group, an informa business

© 2018 Taylor & Francis

All rights reserved. No part of this book may be reprinted or reproduced or utilised in any form or by any electronic, mechanical, or other means, now known or hereafter invented, including photocopying and recording, or in any information storage or retrieval system, without permission in writing from the publishers.

Trademark notice: Product or corporate names may be trademarks or registered trademarks, and are used only for identification and explanation without intent to infringe.

British Library Cataloguing in Publication Data
A catalogue record for this book is available from the British Library

ISBN 13: 978-0-8153-9206-4

Typeset in Myriad Pro
by diacriTech, Chennai

Publisher's Note
The publisher accepts responsibility for any inconsistencies that may have arisen during the conversion of this book from journal articles to book chapters, namely the possible inclusion of journal terminology.

Disclaimer
Every effort has been made to contact copyright holders for their permission to reprint material in this book. The publishers would be grateful to hear from any copyright holder who is not here acknowledged and will undertake to rectify any errors or omissions in future editions of this book.

Contents

	Citation Information	vii
	Notes on Contributors	ix
	Preface	xi
	Peter Gilroy	
	Introduction: Education for purposeful teaching around the world	1
	Kirsi Tirri, Seana Moran and Jenni Menon Mariano	
1	Finnish student teachers' perceptions on the role of purpose in teaching	7
	Kirsi Tirri and Elina Kuusisto	
2	Finnish and Iranian teachers' views on their competence to teach purpose	16
	Elina Kuusisto, Khalil Gholami and Kirsi Tirri	
3	Principles and methods to guide education for purpose: a Brazilian experience	31
	Ulisses F. Araujo, Valeria Amorim Arantes, Hanna Cebel Danza, Viviane Potenza Guimarães Pinheiro and Monica Garbin	
4	The influence of Chinese college teachers' competence for purpose support on students' purpose development	40
	Fei Jiang, Shan Lin and Jenni Menon Mariano	
5	What do teachers think about youth purpose?	57
	Seana Moran	
6	Learning from the wisdom of practice: teachers' educational purposes as pathways to supporting adolescent purpose in secondary classrooms	77
	Brandy P. Quinn	
	Index	99

Citation Information

The chapters in this book were originally published in the *Journal of Education for Teaching*, volume 42, issue 5 (December 2016). When citing this material, please use the original page numbering for each article, as follows:

Preface
Peter Gilroy
Journal of Education for Teaching, volume 42, issue 5 (December 2016) p. 525

Introduction
Education for purposeful teaching around the world
Kirsi Tirri, Seana Moran and Jenni Menon Mariano
Journal of Education for Teaching, volume 42, issue 5 (December 2016) pp. 526–531

Chapter 1
Finnish student teachers' perceptions on the role of purpose in teaching
Kirsi Tirri and Elina Kuusisto
Journal of Education for Teaching, volume 42, issue 5 (December 2016) pp. 532–540

Chapter 2
Finnish and Iranian teachers' views on their competence to teach purpose
Elina Kuusisto, Khalil Gholami and Kirsi Tirri
Journal of Education for Teaching, volume 42, issue 5 (December 2016) pp. 541–555

Chapter 3
Principles and methods to guide education for purpose: a Brazilian experience
Ulisses F. Araujo, Valeria Amorim Arantes, Hanna Cebel Danza, Viviane Potenza Guimarães Pinheiro and Monica Garbin
Journal of Education for Teaching, volume 42, issue 5 (December 2016) pp. 556–564

Chapter 4
The influence of Chinese college teachers' competence for purpose support on students' purpose development
Fei Jiang, Shan Lin and Jenni Menon Mariano
Journal of Education for Teaching, volume 42, issue 5 (December 2016) pp. 565–581

CITATION INFORMATION

Chapter 5

What do teachers think about youth purpose?
Seana Moran
Journal of Education for Teaching, volume 42, issue 5 (December 2016) pp. 582–601

Chapter 6

Learning from the wisdom of practice: teachers' educational purposes as pathways to supporting adolescent purpose in secondary classrooms
Brandy P. Quinn
Journal of Education for Teaching, volume 42, issue 5 (December 2016) pp. 602–623

For any permission-related enquiries please visit:
http://www.tandfonline.com/page/help/permissions

Notes on Contributors

Valeria Amorim Arantes is Associate Professor at the School of Education, University of São Paulo, Brazil.

Ulisses F. Araujo is Full Professor at the University of São Paulo, Brazil. His research interests aim at improvement and innovation in basic and higher education through the articulation between project and problem-based learning, educational technologies, and citizenship commitment.

Hanna Cebel Danza is a project supervisor in the degree in Natural Sciences and Mathematics at UNIVESP, Brazil. She is also a PhD student at the Faculty of Education, University of São Paulo, Brazil.

Monica Garbin is Associate Professor at UNIVESP, Brazil.

Khalil Gholami is Assistant Professor at the Department of Educational Sciences, University of Kurdistan, Iran. He is also a Postdoctoral Researcher at the University of Helsinki, Finland.

Peter Gilroy is the sole editor of the *Journal of Education for Teaching*. He is Professor Emeritus at Manchester Metropolitan University, UK, and holds visiting chairs at Hull, Roehampton, and Plymouth universities.

Fei Jiang is a Lecturer at the Center on Ideological and Political Education, Northeast Normal University, China. Her research interests include moral and civic education in higher education, teacher education, and cross-cultural studies.

Elina Kuusisto is a researcher at the Faculty of Educational Sciences, University of Helsinki, Finland. Currently she is studying school pedagogy, more particularly moral and religious education, teachers' moral competence, purposeful teaching, and talent development.

Shan Lin worked at the School of Math and Statistics and KLASMOE, Northeast Normal University, China.

Jenni Menon Mariano is Associate Professor of Education at the University of South Florida Sarasota-Manatee, USA. She teaches courses in child and adolescent development and learning, moral development and education, classroom assessment, and the psychology of life purpose. Her research examines positive human and community development in multinational contexts. She currently serves on the Executive Board of the Association for Moral Education and reviews for multiple research journals.

NOTES ON CONTRIBUTORS

Seana Moran is Research Assistant Professor of Developmental Psychology at Clark University, USA. Her research focuses on how individuals contribute to collaborations, society, culture, and other institutions, as well as how they come to recognize their actions as contributions to a greater good. More specifically, she writes about the intersections of life purpose, morality/ethics, creativity, culture, and wisdom.

Viviane Potenza Guimarães Pinheiro is Director at Escola Pinheiro, Brazil. Prior to this she acted as a project supervisor at UNIVESP, Brazil.

Brandy P. Quinn is an Assistant Professor in the College of Education at Texas Christian University, USA. In her current research, she investigates whether and how school communities foster in youth the desire and drive to contribute to society through their own gifts and talents.

Kirsi Tirri is a Professor of Education and Research Director at the Helsinki Collegium for Advanced Studies at the University of Helsinki, Finland. She is also a Visiting Professor at St. John's University, USA and University of Tallinn, Estonia. Tirri has been the President of ECHA (European Council for High Ability) for the years 2008–2012, the President of the SIG International Studies at AERA (American Educational Research Association) for the years 2010–2013, and the President of the Finnish Academy of Science and Letters for the years 2016–2017.

Preface

The guest editors for this last issue of JET volume 42 are Kirsi Tirri, Seana Moran and Jenni Menon Mariano from Finland and the USA, respectively. Their proposal for what has become this Special Issue was an intriguing one, as your editor in his ignorance had not realised that in many countries two themes were gaining currency in teacher education, namely 'teaching *for* purpose and teaching *with* purposefulness'. The meaning that might be given to 'purpose' is very much context dependent and so it is appropriate that this Special Issue should draw on a number of social contexts to examine what 'education for purpose' might involve in the different social contexts the contributors represent.

There is much in this Special Issue to consider, not least by your editor. After all, if we are being asked to consider questions such as 'Why do lessons matter?' and 'What are the short and long term impacts of one's teaching on one's pupils and their communities?' then it is but a small step for your editor to ask himself similar 'purpose questions' such as 'Why does JET matter?' and 'What is the short and long term effect of JET on the teacher education community, very broadly defined?'. The possible response would also parallel the answers offered in this issue of the journal, namely that JET provides a platform for high quality international scholarship that engages with and beyond its immediate community, this Special Issue being a fine example of that philosophy in action.

Peter Gilroy

Education for purposeful teaching around the world

Kirsi Tirri, Seana Moran and Jenni Menon Mariano

This special issue researches two themes that are gaining emphasis in teacher education in many countries: teaching *for* purpose and teaching *with* purposefulness. Pupils learn desired qualities via schooling, and teachers facilitate these pupils' learning. According to the papers in this special issue of the *Journal of Education for Teaching*, 'purpose' is a relevant concept to address the concerns of contemporary education. It is important to examine purpose during youth when its propensity for growth first emerges (e.g. Damon, Menon, and Bronk 2003). Some scholars assert the strong potential of formal education for cultivating purpose (e.g. Mariano 2011), but empirical studies show mixed results (Moran et al. 2012).

In recent years, a few scholars have turned their attention to the possibility of multicultural application of purpose for youth development and teacher education (e.g. Bundick and Tirri 2014). The papers in this special issue also support the importance of purpose in youth development, in formal education and in multicultural and multinational contexts.

Purpose may use different words or be defined differently in different languages and cultures. Thus, an aim of this special issue is to consider purpose as a framework for teaching while also exploring insights into purpose's comparative application in diverse educational contexts.

Purpose and purposefulness

In this special issue's conceptualisation, 'purpose' refers to 'a stable and generalised intention to accomplish something that is both meaningful to the self and of intended consequence to the world beyond the self' (Damon, Menon, and Bronk 2003, 121). The degree to which one may be considered purposeful rests on whether one's major life goals focus on making an impact on the world beyond only gratifying one's own needs, and engagement toward actualising those life goals (Bundick and Tirri 2014, 4). This prosocial conceptualisation of purpose extends Frankl's (1988) notions of responsibility and 'giving to the world', which emphasise the essential nature of self-transcendent goals. To this end, a purpose may function not only as a life aim, but as a 'moral beacon' which motivates individuals to commit to and engage in prosocial, generative behaviours across their lifespans.

Purpose in educational context

Teachers aim to create effective, supportive and challenging environments in which pupils can learn skills, dispositions and behaviours to direct their lives successfully. This new educational charter means that education extends beyond acquiring knowledge or increasing cognitive capacities toward developing the whole person, including emotion, motivation, volition, spirituality and sociality (Tirri 2011). This development is not limited to effectiveness within pupils' own cultures, but increasingly as part of a global arena of interwoven cultures. Teachers are particularly important for fostering life purpose among pupils (Tirri 2014; Tirri and Ubani 2013). Teachers provide encouragement, guidance, opportunities to engage and pathways (Koshy and Mariano 2011; Malin et al. 2013; Moran et al. 2012). They are role models and instructors for goal-directedness, planfulness (i.e. future planning) and consideration of the consequences of one's actions, although to different degrees depending on cultural factors (Bundick and Tirri 2014). As the world grows more interconnected through social media, it is important to understand the ways different cultures address educating for purpose.

Purposeful teaching

One of the most important bases for a teacher to have before he or she can be expected to teach for purpose is an understanding of his or her own purpose (Damon 2008). Just as teachers must have some expertise in the content area, they are instructing before they can be expected to effectively disseminate the material and engage the pupils with it, the teachers themselves should have some sense of their own most important life goals and an understanding of how they make meaning of their own lives, before engaging with intentionality in purpose development of their pupils (Bundick and Tirri 2014, 5, 6).

Teachers' visions of ideal school practices may provide ways to access teachers' sense of purpose. Vision can provide inspiration and motivation to teachers and also guide them to reflect on their work (Husu and Tirri 2007; Tirri and Husu 2006). According to Darling-Hammond and Bransford (2000), one of the most powerful predictors of teachers' commitment to teaching is a sense of efficacy, the teachers' sense that they are making a positive difference in the lives of their pupils. For teaching to be purposeful teachers need skills to teach their subject matter, regardless of what it is, in the ways that would open up its educational meaning (Tirri and Ubani 2013). The German *Didaktik* is based on the idea that any given matter can represent many different meanings, and many different matters can open up any given meaning. But there is no matter without meaning, and no meaning without matter (Hopmann 2007, 116). Meaning emerges when the content is enacted in a classroom based on the methodological decisions of a teacher; meaning making is facilitated when teachers provide opportunities for their pupils to reflect upon what is meaningful to them, and how their current engagements are related to their life goals. Through this process, the individual growth of a student is fostered and the potential for purpose development is promoted.

Purposeful teaching around the world

Purpose can be seen as a key promoter in both professional growth and resilience for teachers (Tirri and Ubani 2013). As a result, in many countries around the world, the purpose of education and the role of schools as supports for purpose development are growing as important topics of scientific research and educational debate (e.g. Shin et al. 2013). A conceptual shift is occurring in several countries: the purpose of education is becoming an education for purpose.

In this special issue, researchers around the world examine what a shift toward an education for purpose looks like across several cultures. Many of the authors of these articles are collaborators in a three-year, multinational research study, funded by The John Templeton Foundation, United States, on how educational experiences can help pupils find a strong sense of purpose for their lives. The countries involved are the United States, Brazil, South Korea, China, Spain and Finland.

This special issue is a helpful accessory to the journal's recent special issue on a 40-year retrospective of teacher education (JET 40:5) by turning our eyes to the future: How do teachers foresee their role in the development of youth not just in terms of knowledge but also in terms of their own personal life aims? How do teachers understand their influence on youth's growing 'moral beacon' to contribute something to their communities? How do teachers maintain a reflective stance toward their own professional purposes?

Teachers around the world should be explicitly educated for competencies that make purposeful and purpose-oriented teaching possible. The goal of teacher education is to educate teachers not only to teach knowledge content, but also to reflect on the purposefulness of their teaching: Why do their lessons and activities matter? What immediate impact and long-term effects do their teaching efforts have on the pupils as well as the communities in which pupils interact?

To advance the scientific study of purpose education, the papers in this special issue address several of the most pertinent themes and questions around education for purpose by teachers. How can teachers move from interest to effective action? Based on their experience in Brazil, Araujo, Arantes, Danza, Pinheiro and Garbin explore Problem-Based Learning, Project-Based Learning and Design Thinking principles for purpose interventions that make salient life's uncertainty and complexity and that help pupils realise the impact of their actions on others. In these authors' view, teachers are the 'mediators' between students' in-process purpose growth and the world by helping students create community-serving products.

A common sentiment across papers is that teacher education for purpose can and should begin with teachers' beliefs: What do teachers think about purpose? Does how they think about purpose align with what they think about teaching and about supporting pupils? How does teaching purpose relate to teachers' ethics? Moran's paper and Quinn's paper examine beliefs among American teachers, providing empirical support for what some educators have suspected: even though purpose is not integrated into the public school curriculum, it is on the radar of American teachers' instruction (e.g. Koshy and Mariano 2011). The paper by Kuusisto, Gholami and Tirri finds that the Finnish and Iranian teachers' self ratings of competence were predicted by their higher levels of ethical sensitivity, such as caring about others.

EDUCATION FOR PURPOSEFUL TEACHING AROUND THE WORLD

The two American studies collect data related to the specific dimensions of Damon's (2008) definition of purpose: meaning, intention, engagement and beyond-the-self impact. As Quinn suggests, this dimensional approach may be important when addressing educating for purpose because adolescents likely are at different stages of purpose development. Many may not have all the dimensions integrated yet (Moran 2009). It would be helpful for teachers to understand that these dimensions of purpose may not develop at the same time or rate. Thus, a binary view of whether teachers are or are not addressing the full purpose construct could miss important ways that teachers can address each dimension of purpose. For example, the Finnish and Iranian teachers' ethical sensitivity may be particularly helpful in developing pupils' abilities to find opportunities for beyond-the-self impact.

How well prepared do teachers feel they are to teach purpose? Three papers by Kuusisto, Gholami and Tirri, by Jiang, Lin and Mariano, and by Tirri and Kuusisto explore perceptions of teachers' competence for teaching purpose in Finland, Iran, and China. In all three countries, teaching is considered a moral profession, yet the ways teachers are educated in their profession differences in cultural focus. China has a direct and compulsory, textbook-focused curriculum for 'purpose', whereas teaching purpose is less explicit but still integrated into the philosophy of teaching in the other two countries. These differences in education impact which dimensions of purpose teachers feel most competent to address. For example, Iranians teach reflection on purpose in life and plans for the future, whereas Finnish teachers emphasise the importance and consequences of one's actions and decisions. Teachers in all of the countries rated their competence highly, but Chinese teachers considered themselves significantly *more* competent at providing purpose support to their students than their students thought they were.

Congruence between teacher competence and beliefs, teacher and pupil, teacher and subject matter, and pupil and subject matter arises in all the studies in this issue. Congruence could provide a framework for further research. In particular, can life purpose be used as a 'bridge' between pupils' or student teachers' schooling and their future lives, which can then support their current engagement in coursework (Moran 2014)? For example, Finnish teachers' own purposefulness relates to their competence for teaching purpose, and teachers' purposefulness is associated with pupils' purposefulness. Chinese students who rated their college teachers as supportive of purpose also articulated clear beyond-the-self goals for purpose.

If congruence is important, what is the role of subject matter as a venue for purpose development? Several papers prompt further questions about the relationships among subject matter, teachers' education in that subject matter and teachers' overall teaching competence in pupils' purpose development. Some researchers suggest that some subject areas may be more amenable to teaching purpose than other subject areas. For example, subject areas that address social problems, such as religion or social studies, may make it easier for teachers of these subject areas to feel more competent also teaching purpose. In contrast to mathematics and science teachers in Finland, it would be difficult to imagine religious studies teacher candidates being able to avoid contemplation of purpose and meaning in their own lives, since their subject area demands it. Yet in Finland, the overall philosophy of teacher education does not differ by subject area. And the influence of subject matter may not hold in all cultures. Whereas in Finland and China, competence in teaching purpose related to subject matter, in Iran it was not (see also Tirri 2012).

Increasingly, the development of purpose in young people is gaining traction in education as researchers and educators see purpose as an effective concept for not only academic achievement but civic engagement and good citizenship as well. The interest is not limited to one country or region of the world. This special issue offers a comparative view of teaching purpose in several countries with the hope of launching further interest in making the development of purpose a key educational goal worldwide.

Disclosure statement

No potential conflict of interest was reported by the authors.

References

Bundick, M. J., and K. Tirri. 2014. "Student Perceptions of Teacher Support and Competencies for Fostering Youth Purpose and Positive Youth Development: Perspectives from Two Countries." *Applied Developmental Science* 18 (3): 148–162.

Damon, W. 2008. *The Path to Purpose: Helping our Children Find Their Calling in Life*. New York: Simon & Schuster.

Damon, W., J. Menon, and K. C. Bronk. 2003. "The Development of Purpose During Adolescence." *Applied Developmental Science* 7 (3): 119–128.

Darling-Hammond, L., and J. Bransford. 2000. *Preparing Teachers for a Changing World: What Teachers Should Learn and Be Able to Do*. San Francisco, CA: Jossey-Bass.

Frankl, V. E. 1988. *Man's Search for Meaning*. New York: Pocket Books.

Hopmann, S. 2007. "Restrained Teaching: The Common Core of Didaktik." *European Educational Research Journal* 6 (2): 109–124.

Husu, J., and K. Tirri. 2007. "Developing Whole School Pedagogical Values – A Case of Going through the Ethos of 'Good Schooling'." *Teaching and Teacher Education* 23 (4): 390–401.

Koshy, S. I., and J. M. Mariano. 2011. "Promoting Youth Purpose: A Review of the Literature." *New Directions for Youth Development* 2011 (132): 13–29.

Malin, H., T. S. Reilly, B. Quinn, and S. Moran. 2013. "Adolescent Purpose Development: Exploring Empathy, Discovering Roles, Shifting Priorities, and Creating Pathways." *Journal of Research on Adolescence* 24 (1): 186–199. doi:10.1111/jora.12051.

Mariano, J. M. 2011. "Conclusion: Recommendations for How Practitioners, Researchers, and Policymakers Can Promote Youth Purpose." *New Directions for Youth Development* 2011 (132): 105–111. doi:10.1002/yd.431.

Moran, S. 2009. "Purpose: Giftedness in Intrapersonal Intelligence." *High Ability Studies* 20 (2): 143–159. doi:10.1080/13598130903358501.

Moran, S. 2014. "What 'Purpose' Means to Youth: Are There Cultures of Purpose?" *Applied Developmental Science* 18 (3): 163–175. doi:10.1080/10888691.2014.924359.

Moran, S., M. J. Bundick, H. Malin, and T. S. Reilly. 2012. "How Supportive of Their Specific Purposes Do Youth Believe Their Family and Friends Are?" *Journal of Adolescent Research* 28 (3): 348–377. doi:10.1177/0743558412457816.

Shin, J., H. Hwang, E. Cho, and A. McCarthy-Donovan. 2013. "Current Trends in Korean Adolescents' Social Purpose." *Journal of Youth Development* 9 (2): 16–33.

Tirri, K. 2011. "Holistic School Pedagogy and Values: Finnish Teachers' and Pupils' Perspectives." *International Journal of Educational Research* 50 (2): 159–165.

Tirri, K. 2012. "The Core of School Pedagogy: Finnish Teachers' Views on the Educational Purposefulness of Their Teaching." In *Miracle of Education? Teaching and Learning in Finland*, edited by H. Niemi, A. Toom, and A. Kallioniemi, 55–68. Rotterdam: Sense Publishers.

Tirri, K. 2014. "The Last 40 Years in Finnish Teacher Education." *Journal of Education for Teaching* 40 (5): 600–609. doi:10.1080/02607476.2014.956545.

Tirri, K., and J. Husu. 2006. "Pedagogical Values behind Teachers' Reflection of School Ethos." In *New Teaching and Teacher Issues*, edited by M. Klein, 163–182. New York: Nova Science Publishers.

Tirri, K., and M. Ubani. 2013. "Education of Finnish student teachers for purposeful teaching." *Journal of Education for Teaching* 39 (1): 21–29. doi:10.1080/02607476.2012.733188.

Finnish student teachers' perceptions on the role of purpose in teaching

Kirsi Tirri and Elina Kuusisto

ABSTRACT

This study identifies the nature of the purposes that Finnish student teachers of different subjects ($N = 372$) have for teaching and how these perceptions could inform teacher education. Earlier studies have shown that both American and Finnish students have found the role of their teachers to be very important in teaching and learning purpose. Finnish student teachers have also been found to be purposeful in their teaching. The data for this study were gathered in 2013 with quantitative questionnaires measuring different elements of purpose, such as purpose identification, goal-directedness, beyond-the-self orientation, and competence to teach purpose. Using K-Cluster analysis, four purpose profiles were identified among student teachers: Purposeful, Dabblers, Dreamers, and Disengaged. Student teachers of religious education were found to be the most purposeful in their profiles, while student teachers of mathematics differed from the others, with more than 40% having a Disengaged profile. The results indicate that student teachers of mathematics need special support for their purpose development, as well as education in purposeful teaching.

Introduction

In today's changing world teachers need to foster the holistic development of their students, including in cognitive, social, and moral dimensions. They need to equip their students with a variety of skills and the knowledge required for the future and for life; even more important is the need to nurture students in the ideals of a modern democratic society (Dewey 1927). The societal task of schools is to raise responsible future citizens, and its moral aspect represents a strong and significant dimension of this effort. Teaching is inherently a moral endeavour and should be a central part of teacher education; student teachers should become aware of the nature of this work and of their crucial role in its development (Toom, Husu, and Tirri 2015). For the moral aspect of the work, teachers need a sense of purpose to find their vocations educationally meaningful and to be able to foster purposefulness in their students (Bundick and Tirri 2014). Finnish teacher education has a strong value and knowledge base in the German tradition together with Anglo-American influences. The German *Didaktik* is based on the idea that any given topic can represent many different meanings, and many different topics can illustrate any given meaning. Yet there is no subject without meaning, and no meaning without a subject (Hopmann 2007, 116). Meaning is what emerges when content is expounded in a classroom based on the teacher's methodological decisions. In this process, the teacher fosters the growth of the individual student. Hopmann (2007, 115) describes the process in the following way: 'The purpose of teaching and schooling is in this perspective neither to transport knowledge from society to a learner (curriculum), nor a transposing of knowledge from science or other domains to the classroom, but rather the use of knowledge as a transformative tool of unfolding the learner's individuality and sociability, in short: the 'Bildung' of the learners by teaching'.

The German concept of *Bildung* also refers to the holistic aspect of pedagogy. It includes both the development of an individual's talents and abilities as well as the development of a society. *Bildung* requires a passionate search for continuous individual growth and the ability to engage in the critical development of society in order to actualise the highest ideals.

Educational researchers and practitioners argue that purpose development should be part of schooling (Koshy and Mariano 2011). In Finnish teacher education, the specific aim is to educate autonomous professionals who build their practice on research-based knowledge and ethical values (Tirri 2014). It is an approach that acknowledges the normative nature and context dependency of teaching. The teaching-studying-learning process is guided by the Finnish national curriculum and takes place in an institutional context, usually public schools. Teachers need a sense of purpose for their work in order to be educationally meaningful and to be able to foster purposefulness in their students. American studies show that the most strongly purposeful youth who do mention schooling as an influence often report their teacher as fundamental to the development of their purpose (Bronk 2012; Moran et al. 2012; Malin et al. 2013; Bundick and Tirri 2014). According to Finnish empirical studies, both practicing teachers and student teachers emphasise some *general purposes in teaching*, regardless of the subject matter (Tirri 2012; Tirri and Ubani 2013). All view themselves as responsible professionals whose task is to teach the basic knowledge of their subject. Furthermore, they view themselves as responsible for the holistic education of their students, including the students' personal and ethical growth. Practicing teachers seem to have a stronger emphasis on students than do student teachers, whose main concern is still their own mastery of the subject matter and the educational responsibility involved in teaching.

Some *subject-specific purposes in teaching* were also found. In our empirical studies with Finnish subject-teacher students and practicing subject teachers, the teachers and student teachers of mathematics both emphasise the importance of meeting the needs of different learners, for example, very gifted students and girls (Tirri 2012). Mathematical thinking can be seen as a basic skill in many sciences, and those who teach this subject want to promote that kind of thinking in order to give their students the best chances to succeed in school and beyond.

In previous American studies, young people were broken down into four groups according to their sense of purpose. Damon calls these groups the disengaged and non-purposeful, the dreamers, the dabblers, and the purposeful (Damon 2008, 59). In the context of teaching, *the disengaged* are teachers who express no purpose to their teaching nor do they show any signs that they are seeking purpose. Like the disengaged group in the American studies, some of these Finnish teachers might be detached, while others confine their interests to hedonic or ego-boosting pursuits that show little concern for the world beyond the self. *The dreamers* are teachers who express ideas about purposes that they would like to have, for example, imaginative educational ideas, but who have done little or nothing to try out their ideas. They have idealistic aspirations related to teaching and learning, but have put no practical plans or tests into action to pursue their purpose in a realistic way. *The dabblers* are teachers who have engaged in activities that appear to be at least potentially purposeful, but who show little awareness of the meaning of these activities beyond the present. These teachers also show few signs of committing themselves to such pursuits over time. They often change their teaching method or philosophy of education without any coherent sense of what they want to achieve with their teaching. Their interests are too short-term and changeable to become the basis for purposeful teaching. *The purposeful* are those teachers who have found something meaningful to which to dedicate themselves, who have sustained this interest over a period of time, and who express a clear sense of what they want to accomplish in their teaching and why. They have found an ultimate goal that inspires their teaching efforts from day to day and helps them see the future in their career. These teachers have also taken concrete steps to achieve their ambitions and act according to their educational vision.

Research context: Finnish teacher education

Our sample includes student teachers from kindergarten, classroom and subject teachers' programmes. All universities in Finland have teacher education programmes for classroom teachers and subject teachers, and, since 1995, for kindergarten teachers, who are required to earn a bachelor's degree. Both elementary and secondary school teachers must earn a master's degree, and their academic status is the same. Kansanen (1999) describes the contents of research-based teacher education at the Department of Teacher Education at the University of Helsinki as including three large content areas: pedagogical content knowledge or subject didactics, the theory of education, and practice. These components are in reciprocal interaction, and their main organising theme, from the beginning of the programme to the end, is a research-based approach integrated into every course. Courses in systematic research methods are introduced at the very beginning of their studies. The research-based approach culminates in the writing of a required master's thesis. Class teachers (those teaching grades 1–6, pupils from 7 to 12 years of age) write their theses in the field of education, while subject teachers (who teach grades 7–12, with pupils from 13 to 18 years of age) choose a topic in their major from a subject they are teaching.

Finnish young adults, especially females, have always been interested in being teachers. Teaching has traditionally been a respected occupation in Finland, but more rigorous preparation has actually made it even more attractive to talented students. Today it is easier to be admitted to the faculties of law or medicine at the University of Helsinki than it is to gain admission to the classroom teacher education programme. At the University of Helsinki, fewer than 10% of applicants are accepted annually for classroom teacher education in the Department of Teacher Education. Classroom student teachers study education as their major and are selected on the basis of their academic achievement as well as their communication and social skills. The entrance examination includes written assignments, interviews, and pedagogical assignments. By contrast, the subject teacher applicants apply to the faculties in their respective subjects and choose teacher education later, usually after two years (Kansanen 2003, 87). It is more difficult to be admitted into teacher education in some subjects, such as religious education, than in others, such as mathematics, where there is a shortage of teachers (Tirri and Ubani 2013).

This article reports empirical findings on Finnish student teachers ($N = 372$) who study at the University of Helsinki. The data were gathered with an online purpose survey in 2013 at the beginning of the students' pedagogical studies. Our research questions are:

(1) What purposes do Finnish student teachers perceive in teaching?
(2) How do students in different programmes (kindergarten teachers, elementary school class teachers, and secondary school subject teachers) differ in their perceptions on the role of purpose in teaching?

How can purpose be taught?

Purpose is defined as a stable, long-term goal to contribute to the world beyond a self that is also meaningful to the self (Damon 2008; Damon, Menon, and Cotton Bronk 2003). This multidimensional understanding of purpose prerequisites that a person has searched and found a meaningful life goal (Steger et al. 2006). It also includes that one is committed, engaged and goal-directed in realising the purpose (see e.g. Ryff 1989). Two kinds of goals in life can be identified, one that has as its primary intent the benefit of the world beyond the self (a purpose) and another whose primary intent is to benefit the self (a self-oriented life goal). This conceptualisation of purpose extends Frankl's (1988) notions of responsibility and 'giving to the world,' which emphasise the essential nature of self-transcendent goals to experience purpose in its deepest sense. To this end, a purpose may function not only as a life aim, but also as a 'moral beacon,' which motivates a person to commit to and engage in pro-social, generative behaviours in adolescence and the years to come (Damon 2008). To live purposefully, one must understand their purpose(s) in life, plan and be future-oriented, and believe that one has the capacity to achieve their life's goals.

One of the most important foundations for teaching purpose is a teacher's understanding of their own purpose (Bundick and Tirri 2014). When *teaching purpose* a teacher helps students to find their own purpose in life in subject-matter taught or in life in general. This kind of teaching can be called 'purpose education' and it can be actualised in many ways and in many different contexts. Purposeful teaching, on the other hand, is intentional activity based on formal curriculum in pedagogical institution. In this context the teacher's main task is to build a didactic relation to the student's studying and learning processes. The teacher has the pedagogical and didactic freedom to use the methods with which the meaning of the subject being studied can best be illuminated. The meaning is the key to creating the didactic relation. It also provides the crucial basis for students to study and learn and thereby construct their relationship with the subject content. Thus, different subjects like mathematics, science, social science, languages, or religious education provide the contexts for teaching purpose (see Hopmann 2007). When a teacher illuminates the meaning of a subject, teaching can be described as *purposeful teaching* (Tirri 2012; Tirri and Ubani 2013). Thus, the key for purposeful teaching is a person's ability to illuminate the meaning of a subject and help students create a personal and meaningful relation to that subject. It is plausible that most teachers implicitly engage in *purposeful teaching*, but student teachers especially need education to be able to focus more on supporting the construction of their students' relationship to the subject content rather than on their own relationship to the content.

Data and methods

Participants

The data ($N = 372$) were gathered with an online purpose survey in 2013 at the beginning of Finnish student teachers' pedagogical studies. The student teachers were studying to become kindergarten teachers ($n = 58$), class teachers ($n = 60$), or subject teachers of Finnish ($n = 53$) in foreign languages ($n = 82$), social sciences ($n = 38$), religious education ($n = 29$), or math and science ($n = 52$). Most of the student teachers were females ($n = 288$; 77%). Mean age was 27 years (SD = 7.21).

Instruments

Bundick and Tirri (2014) have operationalised Damon, Menon, and Cotton Bronk's (2003) the purpose construct with three latent variables: a sense of purpose, goal-directedness and a beyond-the-self orientation. A sense of purpose was measured with two subscales, namely, the *presence of purpose* and the *search for purpose*, found on the Meaning in Life Questionnaire (Steger et al. 2006). Both subscales had five items and were rated on a 7-point Likert-type scale (1 = *strongly disagree*, 7 = *strongly agree*). In line with previous studies, the items on both subscales which showed strong reliability as alpha values were *presence of purpose* .728 and *search for purpose* .885. Sample item for presence of purpose include an item such as 'My life has a clear sense of purpose' and for search for purpose an item such as 'I am seeking a purpose or mission for my life.'

To measure *goal-directedness*, a nine-item version of the Purpose in Life subscale of Ryff's Psychological Well-Being measure was utilised (Ryff 1989). Items were rated on a 7-point Likert-type scale (1 = *strongly disagree*, 7 = *strongly agree*), and the alpha value was .784. 'Some people wander aimlessly through life, but I am not one of them' is a good sample item for the measure of goal-directedness.

Beyond-the-self-orientation (BTS) was operationalised with two items measuring social life goals from Roberts and Robins (2000) 'Volunteering in the community' and 'Helping others in need.' Even though there were only two items, the alpha value was .640. The items were rated on a 5-point Likert-type scale in answer to the question: 'How important are the following goals in your life?' (1 = *not important to me* to 5 = *very important to me*).

Furthermore, Bundick and Tirri's (2014) instrument was used to assess student teachers' perceptions of their competence to teach purpose. This measurement is an operationalization of characteristics of predictors of purpose development. The original six items measured students' perceptions of teacher competencies for purpose, and five of the items were modified to fit teachers' self-ratings. The respondents rated the items on a 5-point Likert-type scale (1 = *strongly disagree*, 5 = *strongly agree*). The reliability value of the five items were $\alpha = .633$. Sample items include items such as: 'In my current school, I guide my students to reflect their purpose in life.', 'In my current school, I teach why a lesson or task or experience is important' and 'In my current school, I teach my students how to plan for the future.' Students were advised to answer these questions based on their perceptions on the role of purpose in their teaching and their expectations on their future students.

EDUCATION FOR PURPOSEFUL TEACHING AROUND THE WORLD

Table 1. Clusters of student teachers' purpose profiles.

		Disengaged $n=84$ (23%)	Dreamers $n=54$ (15%)	Dabblers $n=144$ (39%)	Purposeful $n=90$ (24%)	Levene; $F, p,$ η_p^2
Presence of purpose (scale 1–7)	z-scores	−.28 (.87)	−1.40 (.86)	.16 (.70)	.85 (.46)	.000
	M (SD)	4.77 (1.03)	3.45 (1.01)	5.28 (.83)	6.10 (.54)	115.077; .000; .48
Search for purpose (scale 1–7)	z-scores	−52 (.82)	.51 (.77)	.69 (.58)	−.94 (.75)	.001
	M (SD)	3.68 (1.07)	5.01 (1.01)	5.26 (.76)	3.12 (.98)	123.368; .000; .50
Goal-orientation (scale 1–7)	z-scores	−.21 (.77)	−1.51 (.85)	.32 (.67)	.60 (.72)	.308
	M (SD)	5.22 (.57)	4.25 (.63)	5.62 (.50)	5.83 (.54)	108.370; .000; .47
BTS- Social goals (scale 1–5)	z-scores	−.97 (.81)	−.02 (.71)	.30 (.91)	.43 (.85)	.178
	M (SD)	2.33 (.67)	3.12 (.59)	3.39 (.76)	3.49 (.71)	50.630; .000; .29
Competence to teach purpose (scale 1–5)	z-scores	−.98 (.78)	−.33 (.89)	.27 (.81)	.69 (.72)	.186
	M (SD)	3.65 (.38)	3.97 (.44)	4.26 (.40)	4.47 (.36)	73.356; .000; .37

Results

Student teachers' purpose profiles

In order to identify the students' purpose profiles, a cluster analysis was conducted to classify the participants according to their sense of purpose; in other words, the level of presence of purpose, a search for purpose, goal-directedness, beyond-the-self-orientation (BTS), and competence for teaching purpose. A Quick Cluster Analysis with a K-means algorithm was utilised to form clusters. A four-cluster solution was selected, since it provided theoretically sound groups (Naes, Brockhoff, and Tomic 2010). Clusters were labelled according to the score means in line with Damon's (2008, 59–60) qualifications as (1) dabblers, (2) purposeful, (3) disengaged, and (4) dreamers. The profiles differed statistically significantly on clustering variables with effect size ranging from .29 to .50 (Table 1). Games-Howell's and Tukey's pair-wise comparisons revealed that the profiles differed statistically significantly ($p < .05$) with the following exceptions: On *search for purpose*, dreamers and dabblers did not differ from each other ($p = .353$); on *BTS orientation* purposeful and dabblers did not differ ($p = .60$), nor did dreamers and dabblers ($p = .087$).

Figure 1 illustrates the profiles of the four clusters. *Purposeful* student teachers (24%) scored highest in presence of purpose and lowest in search for purpose, indicating that they had found their purpose in life and thus were no longer searching for it. They were also highly goal-directed and committed to realising their purpose, as well as being oriented toward others. Moreover, purposeful student teachers saw themselves as more competent than other groups to teach purpose to their students. The *Dreamers'* (15%) profile was almost the opposite of *Purposeful*, because the Dreamers scored lowest of all groups on presence of purpose and goal-directedness, which means that they had not found their purpose and thus they could not be committed to actualizing it. Instead, Dreamers were strongly seeking purpose and seemed to hope to find something enduring. Dreamers had to some extent beyond-the-self orientation, but they did not feel competent to teach purpose to their students.

Dabblers (39%) shared features with both the Purposeful and Dreamers, since they scored high on all elements of purpose. Dabblers had found a purpose and were committed to its

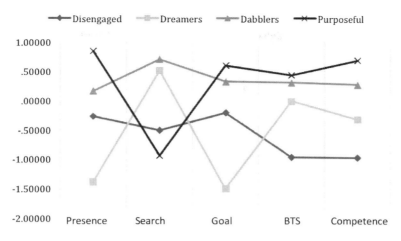

Figure 1. Student teachers' purpose profiles and means of z-scores.

implementation, yet they wanted to keep their options open and continue to search for new possibilities. Dabblers, like Purposeful student teachers, had a beyond-the-self orientation as well as a capacity to teach purpose to their students. *Disengaged* student teachers (23%) had not found their purpose, they were not searching for it, and their goal-directedness was also relatively low. Further, disengaged student teachers were the group least interested in social goals and thus lowest in beyond-the-self orientation and in competence to teach purpose.

The purpose profiles were found to be associated with student teachers' study programmes (χ^2 (18) = 33.283, p = .015). Figure 2 shows that most of the student teachers, regardless of their programmes, were dabblers. However, student teachers of mathematics and science and those teaching religious education differed from the other groups: 38% of the religious education student teachers were found to be purposeful, while over 40% of math and science student teachers had a purpose profile of disengagement, indicating that they did not have strong purpose-related visions, activities, or the confidence to teach purpose.

Discussion

This paper has investigated the various purposes that Finnish student teachers of different subjects have in teaching. The aim for Finnish teacher education is to educate autonomous teachers who have clear goals and a sense of long-term purpose in their work. Education for this kind of purposeful teaching includes opening up the meaning in each subject matter taught and guiding teachers to reflect on their teaching interests, something that could sustain them over a period of time. Education for purposeful teaching also includes discussions and reflections on the ultimate goal in teaching, which inspires teachers from day to day and helps them see the future in their career. The empirical findings among the Finnish student teachers (N = 372) indicate that the majority of them can be profiled as dabblers, persons who think they have found a purpose in their teaching, but are still open to new ideas and ready to change their teaching goals and aims. This open attitude encourages the kind of teacher education in which purpose is discussed with the dabblers and reflected on,

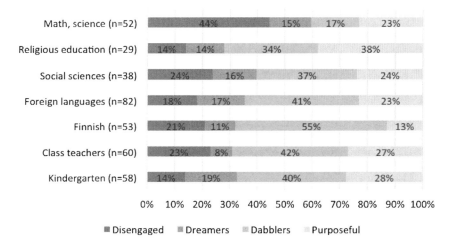

Figure 2. Finnish student teachers' purpose profiles and study programmes.

with the goal of guiding them toward long-term purposeful teaching. The second biggest group among the Finnish student teachers was the purposeful, those who had found a long-term goal and had a commitment to teaching. This is a very encouraging finding and reflects the high quality of the student population in Finland admitted to teacher education departments. The majority of this group viewed teaching both as a good profession and as a calling (Tirri, Husu, and Kansanen 1999).

In our sample, the student teachers of religious education most often demonstrated a purposeful profile, while student teachers of mathematics and science were mostly profiled as disengaged, indicating that they had no strong purpose-related visions, activities, or confidence in teaching purpose. This result supports our previous studies of student teachers and practicing teachers of religious education and mathematics in which similar trends were found (Tirri and Ubani 2013). The smallest group among the student teachers in this study was the dreamers, who were still searching for their teaching purpose. To meet the needs of this group, every study programme, from kindergarten to adult education, should implement education for purposeful teaching.

Both American and Finnish studies among students and teachers indicate that a teacher is a central figure in the purpose development of the youth. Moreover, the moral nature of teaching calls for purposeful teachers for our schools worldwide. This trend also challenges education for teaching all over the world to provide more pre-service and in-service education in purposeful teaching.

Disclosure statement

No potential conflict of interest was reported by the authors.

References

Bronk, K. C. 2012. "A Grounded Theory of the Development of Noble Youth Purpose." *Journal of Adolescent Research* 27 (1): 78–109.

Bundick, M., and K. Tirri. 2014. "Teacher Support and Competencies for Fostering Youth Purpose and Psychological Well-being: Perspectives from Two Countries." *Applied Developmental Science* 18 (3): 148–162. doi:10.1080/10888691.2014.924357.

Damon, W. 2008. *The Path to Purpose*. New York: Free Press.

Damon, W., J. M. Menon, and K. Cotton Bronk. 2003. "The Development of Purpose during Adolescence." *Applied Developmental Science* 7 (3): 119–128. doi:10.1207/S1532480XADS0703_2.

Dewey, J. 1927. "The Public and Its Problems." In *Reprinted in John Dewey, the Later Works: 1925–1953 (LW)*. Vol. 2, edited by J. A. Boydston, 253–372. Carbondale: Southern Illinois University Press.

Frankl, V. E. 1988. *Man's Search for Meaning*. New York: Pocket Books.

Hopmann, S. 2007. "Restrained Teaching: The Common Core of Didaktik." *European Educational Research Journal* 6 (2): 109–124.

Kansanen, P. 1999. "Research-based Teacher Education." In *Teacher Education for Changing School*, edited by J. Hytönen, C. Razdevëek Puko, and G. Smith, 135–141. Ljubljana: University of Ljubljana.

Kansanen, P. 2003. "Teacher Education in Finland: Current Models and New Developments." In *Institutional Approaches to Teacher Education within Higher Education in Europe: Current Models and New Developments*, edited by B. Moon, L. Vlăsceanu and C. Barrows, 85–108. Bucharest: UNESCO-CEPES.

Koshy, S. I., and J. M. Mariano. 2011. "Promoting Youth Purpose: A Review of the Literature." *New Directions for Youth Development* 2011: 13–29. doi:10.1002/yd.425.

Malin, H., T. S. Reilly, B. Quinn, and S. Moran. 2013. "Adolescent Purpose Development: Exploring Empathy, Discovering Roles, Shifting Priorities, and Creating Pathways." *Journal of Research on Adolescence* 24 (1): 186–199. doi:10.1111/jora.12051.

Moran, S., M. J. Bundick, H. Malin, and T. S. Reilly. 2012. "How Supportive of Their Specific Purposes Do Youth Believe Their Family and Friends Are?" *Journal of Adolescent Research* 28 (3): 348–377. doi:10.1177/0743558412457816.

Naes, T., P. B. Brockhoff, and O. Tomic. 2010. "Cluster Analysis: Unsupervised Classification." In *Statistics for Sensory and Consumer Science*, 249–261. John Wiley & Sons Ltd.

Roberts, B. W., and R. W. Robins. 2000. "Broad Dispositions, Broad Aspirations: The Intersection of Personality Traits and Major Life Goals." *Personality and Social Psychology Bulletin* 26 (10): 1284–1296.

Ryff, C. D. 1989. "Happiness is Everything, or is It? Explorations on the Meaning of Psychological Well-being." *Journal of Personality and Social Psychology* 57 (6): 1069–1081.

Steger, M. F., P. Frazier, S. Oishi, and M. Kaler. 2006. "The Meaning in Life Questionnaire: Assessing the Presence of and Search for Meaning in Life." *Journal of Counseling Psychology* 53 (1): 80–93.

Tirri, K. 2012. "The Core of School Pedagogy: Finnish Teachers' Views of the Educational Purposefulness of Their Teaching." In *Miracle of Education*, edited by H. Niemi. A. Toom, and A. Kallioniemi, 55–66. Rotterdam: Sense Publishers.

Tirri, K. 2014. "The Last 40 Years in Finnish Teacher Education." *Journal of Education for Teaching* 40 (5): 600–609. doi:10.1080/02607476.2014.956545.

Tirri, K., J. Husu, and P. Kansanen. 1999. "The Epistemological Stance between the Knower and the Known." *Teaching and Teacher Education* 15 (8): 911–922.

Tirri, K., and M. Ubani. 2013. "Education of Finnish Student Teachers for Purposeful Teaching." *Journal of Education for Teaching* 39 (1): 21–29. doi:10.1080/02607476.2012.733188.

Toom, A., J. Husu, and K. Tirri. 2015. "Cultivating Student Teachers' Moral Competencies in Teaching during Teacher Education." In *International Teacher Education: Promising Pedagogies*. Vol. 3, edited by C. Craig and L. Orland-Barak, 13–31. Bingley: Emerald Group Publishing.

Finnish and Iranian teachers' views on their competence to teach purpose

Elina Kuusisto, Khalil Gholami and Kirsi Tirri

ABSTRACT

This paper examines Finnish ($n = 464$) and Iranian ($n = 556$) teachers' views on their competence to teach purpose. 'Purpose' is defined as a stable intention to accomplish something that is both meaningful to the self and of consequence beyond the self over time. The study revealed that all Iranian teachers evaluated their competence for teaching purpose as being high, regardless of the subject taught. In contrast, among Finnish teachers, there were statistically significant relationships between the subject taught and teachers' self-perceptions: religious education seemed to provide a subject in which Finnish teachers can guide students to consider explicitly their purpose in life and plans for the future, while science and mathematics appeared to offer the most challenging contexts for teaching purpose. Hence, the results challenge Finnish in-service and pre-service teacher education programmes to create new approaches and new cultures for mathematics and science education, which intentionally take into account the moral aspects of teaching. Moreover, regression analysis revealed that teachers' ethical sensitivity predicted their views on teaching purpose in both countries. Results indicate that improving teachers' ethical sensitivity skills in teacher education programmes could provide a significant path for supporting teachers' competence in teaching purpose.

Introduction

> It is our responsibility as adults in this uncertain, confusing, and increasingly cynical time to provide the younger generation with far-horizon guidance. (Damon 2008, 118)

The aim of this study was to examine Finnish and Iranian teachers' ($n = 1020$) views of their competence to teach purpose. The notion of 'purpose' can be seen as the most profound phenomenon of human experience, since it gives reasons not only for acting ethically, but also for living (Bronk 2014; Moran 2009). Today, a general lack of purpose is associated with the stress that people are experiencing and with apathy in the young (Damon 2008).

Research on the subject of purpose peaked for the first time in the 1960s, but it was not until the early 2000s that interest on purpose emerged in connection with the positive psychology movement. So far, recent theories of positive psychology have all found purpose to be the core component of human well-being and positive youth development (Bronk 2014). However, teaching purpose in school and in teacher education programmes has not been extensively studied as yet, while instructional approaches to purpose studies have been neglected (Koshy and Mariano 2011; Mariano 2014). Thus, the main application of the study is to integrate teaching purpose into teacher education programmes as well as into teacher professional development.

In this study, purpose is defined as 'a stable intention to accomplish something that is both meaningful to the self and of consequence beyond the self over time' (Damon, Menon, and Bronk 2003, 212). Within this theoretical framework, education for a purpose is based on the following assumptions: purpose can be taught, everyone can find a purpose (Benson 2006; Damon 2008) and teachers play a crucial role in development of youth purpose (Bundick and Tirri 2014; Damon 2009; Mariano et al. 2011).

According to Koshy and Mariano (2011), there are two different approaches to teaching purpose in a school environment: long-term engagement with purpose-related curricula and one-lesson or one-classroom approaches. The first approach means that instruction in purpose is integrated into all teaching and the teachers' task is to assist students in finding the relevance of the subject (Kansanen and Meri 1999; Tirri and Kuusisto Forthcoming; Ubani 2013). The second approach (the one-lesson or one-classroom approach) refers to classes in which purpose itself is the subject or content of the lesson. This approach is more natural in subjects such as religious education, ethics or philosophy in which religions, worldviews, values, beliefs, ethics and life questions are studied per se and purpose and meaning in life is considered explicitly (Niemi 1987; Ubani 2013).

At least four elements have been identified in previous studies as important in teaching purpose. First, students benefit if they are asked about, guided to reflect on and talk explicitly about, their purposes in life, their core values, and their most important life goals (Bundick 2011). By *discussing purpose*, a teacher may set an example and serve as a role model of an adult who is able to identify, negotiate and verbalise profound and fundamental questions about life (Malin et al. 2014, 195). Furthermore, purpose discussions seem to have lasting psychological advantages, such as increased goal directedness and life satisfaction (Bundick 2011). Second, when a teacher promotes and *teaches future planning* and general future orientation in students, the teacher is helping the students build foundational skills in purpose, namely, goal-setting and intentional engagement (Bundick and Tirri 2014; Nurmi 1991). Third, purpose development is enhanced by *teaching consequences*. Teachers should especially ask students to consider consequences of their actions, thereby guiding the students to develop reflective skills, as well as empathic and pro-social capabilities (Damon 2008). Fourth, teachers need to *teach importance* by guiding students to see the relevance of school in their lives, so that schooling is appreciated and seen as important (Damon 2009; Ubani 2013). Thus, teachers spend time highlighting and explaining to students why school and its tasks are significant and what is the meaning of the school and the subjects studied (see also Tirri and Kuusisto Forthcoming).

Based on the above-mentioned findings, Bundick and Tirri (2014) developed an instrument with which they studied US and Finnish student perceptions of teacher support. The results showed that teachers play an important role in fostering purpose in secondary school students and also that there were important cultural differences in the way purpose is usually fostered (Bundick and Tirri 2014, 158). In the USA, teachers' general support was associated with *teaching future planning*, *consequences* of actions and the *importance* of schooling, of which the last, teaching importance, was related to purpose identification, goal-directedness and beyond-the-self orientation; in other words, dimensions of the definition by Damon, Menon, and Bronk (2003). In Finland general teacher support was associated with *teaching consequences* and *teaching importance*, but not with teaching future planning. However, interestingly, perceived *teaching for planfulness* (that is, future planning) was the element that supported all three dimensions of purpose among Finnish students. Another remarkable aspect of Bundick and Tirri's (2014) study is that the element of *discussing purpose* was not included in either the USA or the Finnish model, which could indicate that purpose in life may not be addressed explicitly by American or Finnish teachers.

This study utilises Bundick and Tirri's (2014) instrument to explore teachers' views on how they support students' purpose in their classrooms. It investigates and compares self-estimations of teachers from a Western country, Finland, and an eastern country, Iran.

Teaching as a moral profession in Finland and Iran

Finland and Iran provide intriguing contexts for this study. In both cultures, the nurturing of virtues and concern with the quality of life are respected (Hofstede, Hofstede, and Minkov 2010). Hence, teaching is valued and is viewed as a moral profession (Gholami, Kuusisto, and Tirri 2015). In Finland, every teacher is understood to be a holistic and moral educator (Tirri 2011, 2012). Similarly, in Iran the moral competencies of teachers are highlighted (Molaiinejad and Zakavati 2008).

Empirical studies exploring Finnish and Iranian teachers' ethical sensitivity have shown that teachers from both countries estimated their ethical sensitivity to be high, indicating that they feel competent to recognise ethical problems and to visualise alternative courses of action in response to ethical situations (Gholami and Tirri 2012; Kuusisto, Tirri, and Rissanen 2012). Further, path analysis revealed that in both groups 'caring about others' was identified as a core element and a culture-invariant aspect of ethical sensitivity (Gholami, Kuusisto, and Tirri 2015). However, cultural differences were evident in the patterns with which Iranian and Finnish teachers construct and understand the prerequisites for caring. In the Finnish case, 'taking the perspective of others' was a strong predictor of 'caring about others' and had a direct effect on this dimension, whereas this was not the situation with the Iranian teachers (ibid.). The results indicate that in a culture with small power distances between pupils and teachers and individualistic values such as Finland's (Hofstede, Hofstede, and Minkov 2010), teachers respect the perspective of others in social interactions. This is in line with Finnish teacher education, which aims to educate autonomous professionals who are able to create a didactic relationship with their students, meaning that a teacher knows their students and is able to provide support and guidance that takes into account the students' individual development (Kansanen and Meri 1999). In contrast, in Iran, which has a large power distance between its teachers and students and a collectivistic culture, accepting collective Islamic values and meanings seems to be a priority in social interactions (Hofstede, Hofstede, and Minkov 2010). As a result, in many social conflicts 'individual agency' and people with secular values are ignored, while the 'collective structure' and individuals having a sacred orientation are acknowledged (Gholami, Kuusisto, and Tirri 2015). In line with these findings, this study investigates how such high ethical sensitivity and moral caring in both contexts is represented in teachers' competence to teach purpose. Thus, the research questions of this study are as follows:

EDUCATION FOR PURPOSEFUL TEACHING AROUND THE WORLD

(1) How do Finnish and Iranian teachers perceive their competence for teaching purpose?
(2) Are there differences between Finnish and Iranian teachers' views whenever their subject of instruction is taken into account?
(3) To what extent does ethical sensitivity predict teaching purpose in each country?

By answering these questions, the present investigation provides information about teachers' views on their competence to teach purpose in two different cultures. Further, this study illustrates which aspects in purpose teaching can be identified as current challenges that need to be addressed in teacher education programmes.

Research contexts: Finnish and Iranian educational systems

Educational policies in Finland and Iran

From the historical point of view, both in Finland and Iran, religion, specifically Lutheran Christianity and Islam respectively, has been intertwined with the development of educational systems (Hedayati et al. 2016; Tirri 2014). However, the role of religion in educational policies has been quite the reverse, as shown in Table 1.

The basis for the modern Iranian educational system was created during the Qajar Dynasty (1794–1925), after which the Pahlavi Dynasty modernised, secularised and Westernised education during the years 1925–1979. This process changed dramatically in 1979 when the Cultural Revolution induced the Islamisation of Iranian society (Cheng and Beigi 2012; Hedayati et al. 2016). As a result, all educational elements and contents that were identified as secular or Western were removed and replaced with Islamic views. Accordingly, the internalisation of Islamic values and ethics was placed among the core aims and content of all education, as well as being among the main professional requirements for teachers, regardless of the level or the subject taught (Hedayati et al. 2016). This also meant that different cultural, ethnic, religious and language backgrounds were intentionally disregarded, as the aim of the Iranian school system was to provide one specific model for educating Islamic Iranian citizens (Cheng and Beigi 2012; Hedayati et al. 2016; Kheiltash and Rust 2009). Islamisation also mandated the educational decision-making process to become highly centralised and was firmly guided by the Iranian Ministry of Education. For example, the Ministry selects the student teachers and employs graduated teachers (Hedayati et al. 2016). Governmentally supervised textbooks are considered the main medium for delivering standardised instruction, as the contents of textbooks create the exclusive basis for national examinations at the conclusion of each level of basic education (Soltan Zadeh 2012).

The year 2010 marked the beginning of a decade of renewal in the Iranian educational system: in 2012 the Ministry specified for the first time in written form the theoretical foundation of Iranian education by publishing *Theoretical Foundation of Fundamental Transformation in the Educational System of the Islamic Republic of Iran* (hereafter IRI) (Hedayati et al. 2016; TFFTES 2012). This document included five sections: (1) Philosophy of Education in IRI, (2) Philosophy of Official and General Education in IRI, (3) Guide for the Educational System in the IRI, (4) Fundamental Transformation in the Educational System of the IRI and (5) the National Curriculum. The basic education system or K-12 was declared to be comprised of primary school (grades 1–6, from the age of six), lower secondary school (grades 7–9), and upper secondary school with academic and vocational sections (grades 10–12).

19

EDUCATION FOR PURPOSEFUL TEACHING AROUND THE WORLD

Table 1. Periods of educational policies in Iran and Finland.

	Iran	Finland
The beginnings	SECULAR EDUCATION Qajar Dynasty: basis for modern Iranian educational system created (1794–1925)	CHRISTIAN EDUCATION Formation of the education system in Sweden–Finland (–1808), Establishment of a university (1640); First curriculum (1649)
	Persian constitutional revolution (1905–1907), establishment of National Parliament, primary school became compulsory, teacher education and sending students to European universities approved	Building the nation with *Bildung* Finland as an Autonomous Grand Duchy of the Russian Empire (1808/1809–1917), first professor in education (1852), secondary teacher education moved to universities, national board of education and matriculation examination (est. 1860s)
	Pahlavi Dynasty: modernisation, secularisation and Westernisation of educational system (1925–1979), shift from a European system to the American one	The independent nation-state (1917) • School for all (1921) • Religious education at the core of the curriculum • Teachers as religious and moral examples 'candles of the nation'
1970	ISLAMISATION OF EDUCATION Islamic Cultural Revolution (1979) Building the nation with *Pure Life* Supreme Council of Cultural Revolution to 'transform universities, schools, cultural and art centres based on Islamic criterion and to spread and reinforce them for educating professors, teachers and mentors who believe in Islam and the independence of the country' (Goals and tasks of Supreme Council of Cultural Revolution 1985)	SECULARISATION OF EDUCATION Equality as a core value Basic education via comprehensive school (1968/1972): primary school (grades 1–6, from the age of 7), lower secondary school (grades 7–9). Voluntary education: upper secondary school (academic orientation, 3 years), vocational school (2–3 years), higher education Class teacher education moved to universities (1974), master's degree minimum for class and subject teachers
1980–1990	CENTRALISATION OF EDUCATION • Islamic values as the main principle of schooling and teacher education • Ministry of Education as supervisor	DECENTRALISATION OF EDUCATION • Individualism and equality as main principles • National Core Curriculum provides general guidelines for municipalities and schools • Teachers' professional ethical code (1998)
2000–2010	CODIFICATION OF ISLAMISATION • *Theoretical Foundation of Fundamental Transformation in the Educational System of the Islamic Republic of Iran* (2012) • Basic education: primary school (grades 1–6, from the age of 6), lower secondary school (grades 7–9), upper secondary school (grades 10–12) • Uniform teacher education: Farhangian University, bachelor's degree minimum for class teachers, master's for subject teachers	TOWARDS GLOBALLY ORIENTATED ETHICAL CITIZENSHIP • Finnish youth's success in PISA studies (2004, 2011) • Research-based teacher education • National Core Curriculum for Basic Education (2014) to be implemented in autumn 2016

Moreover, the minimum degree required for teaching in primary school became a bachelor's degree and in secondary school, a master's. However, for schools in remote and deprived places, primary school teachers with associate degrees and secondary school teachers with bachelor's degrees could be employed as long as they improved their degree qualifications by participating in in-service education (Hedayati et al. 2016). Furthermore, in 2012 Farhangian University (a teacher education university) was established to combine all pre-viously separate and independent teacher education units into one umbrella organisation supervised by the ministry (Hedayati et al. 2016).

Initially, the Finnish educational system had been formed by religious institutions, first the Catholic Church and later the Evangelical Lutheran Church. As early as the 1500s, literacy was a requirement for marriage within the Lutheran Church (Niemi 2012, 21). By the late

1800s, Finnish society began to take responsibility for basic education, and several educational institutions were established; secondary school teacher education was moved to universities, class teacher education began in teacher training colleges, a national board of education was created and a national matriculation examination was composed (Tirri 2014; Uljens and Nyman 2013). In 1921, education for all children became compulsory. Besides teaching skills in reading, writing and calculating, Christianity and practical skills such as handicrafts were the foundations of basic education and also of class teacher education (Tirri 2014). Furthermore, teachers were understood to be religious and moral examples, 'candles of the nation' (Niemi 2012). In the 1960s and 1970s, increasing secularisation and the rise of social democratic values of equality led to the establishment of a nine-year comprehensive school, which replaced the previous parallel school system. Thus, Finnish basic education came to consist of primary school (grades 1–6, from the age of 7) and lower secondary school (grades 7–9, with an optional 10th grade). The Finnish government's principle of 'Equal opportunity and high-quality education for all' meant that education at all levels, including basic education, upper secondary school education (with academic or vocational sections) and higher education became free of charge to every pupil (Tirri and Kuusisto 2013). Furthermore, the education of teachers was strengthened when class teacher education was moved to the universities in 1974, and both class teachers and subject teachers were required to earn a master's degree (Tirri 2014).

In the 1990s, individualism and decentralisation became the prevailing ideas in the Finnish educational system (see Table 1). The role of the national curriculum changed in favour of providing the value basis and general guidelines for municipalities and schools, which in turn create their own specialised curricula with the assistance of teachers (Tirri and Kuusisto 2013). Teachers' pedagogical freedom was emphasised in choosing class content and methods as long as the choices were in line with the National Core Curriculum (Kansanen et al. 2000). Also the Finnish professional ethics code for teachers formalised in 1998 stressed the worth of individuals and the principle of accepting learners as unique, as well as the importance of respecting their rights (*Teacher's Professional Ethics And Ethical Principles's* 2010). Thus, individualism meant that pupils' personal characteristics, needs and interests, as well as the languages and religions of minorities were considered in the National Core Curriculum and thereby in teaching more than in previous decades (Holm and Londen 2010; Poulter 2013). For example, in Finnish schools, language instruction by a native speaker is provided in over 50 languages for students with an immigrant background (*Finnish National Board of Education* 2013), and religious education is arranged in 13 different religions or denominations (*Finnish National Board of Education* 2006). However, at the national level, 92% of basic education students attend religious education classes in Lutheranism, 3% attend classes in other religions and 5% choose secular ethics (Kumpulainen 2015, 22).

Bildung and Pure Life as the ultimate goals of education in Finland and Iran

In Finland and Iran, the ultimate goals of education are *Bildung* (Uljens and Nyman 2013) and *Pure Life* (Hedayati et al. 2016), respectively (see Table 1), topics that offer strong ethical perspectives on teaching, studying and learning. The concept of *Bildung* stems from the German tradition of *Didactics*, meaning 'grasping as much of the world as possible' and 'contributing to humankind' by developing one's unique self (Hopmann 2007, 115). *Bildung*, in other words, requires a passionate search for continuous individual growth and the ability to engage in the critical development of society in order to actualise the highest ideals. *Bildung* has been identified as a key component of Finnish education and nation building since the nineteenth century (Uljens and Nyman 2013). Over the years, the interpretation of *Bildung* has gradually changed from religiously focused obedience to ethically responsible citizenship (Poulter 2013; Uljens and Nyman 2013). The current understanding of *Bildung* has been embodied in the Basic Education Act (628/1998, Section 2) and the *National Core Curriculum for Basic Education* (2014), which define the main goals of education as follows: (1) to support students' holistic growth as human beings and ethically responsible citizens, (2) to provide necessary knowledge and skills and (3) to advance equality and lifelong learning.

In the Iranian context, *Pure Life*, one of the essential concepts in Islamic texts, creates the basis for all education (Hedayati et al. 2016). TFFTES (2012) says, 'the ultimate aim of education in an Islamic society is to prepare students individually and collectively for conscious voluntary pure life in all dimensions', these being religious and moral, physical, social and political, economic and professional, scientific and technological, aesthetic and artistic (Hedayati et al. 2016). *Pure Life* means serving Islam holistically in a categorical and collective way (Kheiltash and Rust 2009; Mehran 2003); in other words, Iranian education aims to educate 'a new generation of pious Muslims with a strong sense of an Iranian-Islamic identity' (Mehran 2003, 326; see also Paivandi 2012).

In both countries, the aims of education create a strong ethical ethos in which every teacher, regardless of school level or subject of instruction, is seen as being morally responsible for the students' holistic growth and well-being. These are courses of conduct that are not self-evident in many countries, such as the Netherlands (Kuusisto et al. Forthcoming). However, the role of religion differs considerably in the Finnish and Iranian educational systems. In Iran, education is strongly religiously orientated, and religion and religious education are explicitly integrated into all teaching (Hedayati et al. 2016). In contrast, in Finnish schools the holistic role of religion has faded, and religions and worldviews are taught mainly in religious education classes.

The above-described theoretical framework, educational contexts and ultimate goals show that, on the one hand, teaching is seen as a moral profession in both Iran and Finland, and helping students find meaning in their academic and personal lives can be considered a moral dimension of teaching. However, on the other hand, the educational philosophies of the educational systems differ in these countries, and thus, Finnish and Iranian teachers are most likely to deal with teaching purpose in different ways. In other words, teachers in Finland and Iran provide distinct horizons for students to follow in school. This study gains insight into how such different contexts are associated with teachers' views on teaching purpose.

Data and methods

Participants

The Finnish data were gathered from teachers working in comprehensive school or upper secondary school. Principals ($n = 370$) were approached via email in seven Finnish cities (Helsinki, Espoo and Vantaa in the Helsinki metropolitan area; Tampere and Jyväskylä in central Finland; Joensuu in eastern Finland; and Oulu in northern Finland). They were asked to forward an invitation to their teachers to complete an electronic version of a questionnaire.

Only 11 principals in 3 different cities informed us that they had in fact forwarded the questionnaire. However, a few principals from four other cities also informed their teachers about the study, because the 83 teachers (18%) who offered their email addresses as a sign of willingness to be interviewed represented all 7 cities. The Finnish sample consisted of practising teachers ($n = 464$) who worked as primary school class teachers ($n = 166$), as well as lower and upper secondary school subject teachers ($n = 298$). The latter taught science ($n = 64$), social science ($n = 34$), languages ($n = 64$), religious education ($n = 38$) and other subjects (e.g. art, home economics, crafts and physical education) ($n = 98$). The majority were females ($n = 350$), with a minority of males ($n = 114$). The Finnish sample included teachers with the following years of experience: 1–4 ($n = 61$), 5–9 ($n = 90$), 10–14 ($n = 74$), 15–19 ($n = 62$) and over 20 ($n = 177$).

The Iranian data were collected from teachers in Kurdistan at three levels of K-12 education. Kurdistan is one of 31 provinces in Iran and has about one and half million inhabitants, the majority of whom have a Kurdish ethnic background. A total of 600 primary, middle and high-school teachers were asked to participate in our study on a voluntary basis. One of the researchers (of Iranian origin) was granted permission to visit the site to collect the data. The researcher personally visited each of the 21 schools that volunteered to participate in the study and delivered hard copies of the same questionnaire that was given to Finnish teachers, albeit in translation into Farsi. These questionnaires were given to the principal of each school for distribution to the Iranian teachers. When the questionnaires were returned, it was found that some 44 cases had significant missing data, and these were excluded from our analysis. The final Iranian sample ($n = 556$) consisted of males ($n = 332$) and females ($n = 224$) who represented teaching experiences of 1–4 years ($n = 61$), 5–9 years ($n = 109$), 10–14 years ($n = 147$), 15–19 years ($n = 128$) and over 20 years ($n = 133$). The Iranian teachers worked as primary school class teachers ($n = 125$), as well as lower and upper secondary school subject teachers ($n = 431$). The latter taught science ($n = 101$), social science ($n = 85$), languages ($n = 66$), religious education ($n = 69$) and other subjects (e.g. art, physical education) ($n = 110$).

Instruments

Teachers' evaluations of their competence to teach purpose was assessed with a Bundick and Tirri (2014) instrument, which is an operationalisation of characteristics of predictors of purpose development. The original items measured students' perceptions of teacher competencies for purpose, and they were modified to fit the teachers' self-ratings (Table 2). Items were responded to on five-point Likert-type scale (1 = strongly disagree, 5 = strongly agree). The reliability value of the four items indicated good internal consistency ($a = 716$). Four core dimensions of the Ethical Sensitivity Scale Questionnaire (Gholami, Kuusisto, and Tirri 2015; Tirri and Nokelainen 2011) were utilised as a predictors of teachers' competence to teach purpose. The dimensions were: (1) *taking the perspective of others* (TPO, $a = .724$), (2) *caring by connecting with others* (CCO, $a = .724$), (3) *reading ethical issues* (REI, $a = .599$) and (4) *identifying the consequences of action and options* (ICAO, $a = .724$). Each included four items and were evaluated on a Likert-type scale (1 = strongly disagree, 5 = strongly agree). Sample items include 'I also get along with people who do not agree with me'; 'I take care of the well-being of others and try to improve it'; 'I notice that there are ethical issues involved in human interaction'; and 'I contemplate the consequences of my actions when making ethical decisions'.

EDUCATION FOR PURPOSEFUL TEACHING AROUND THE WORLD

Table 2. Means and standard deviations of Finnish and Iranian teachers' perceptions of their competence to teach purpose.

Dimension and items	M (SD)	Finnish n = 464 M (SD)	Iranian n = 556 M (SD)	t(df), p
Competence to teach purpose	4.24 (.53)	4.15 (.53)	**4.31 (.53)**	−4.859(1018), .000
In my current school…				
• I guide my students to reflect on their purpose in life	4.15 (.86)	3.83 (.91)	**4.42 (.71)**	−11.387(862.513), .000
• I teach my students how to plan for the future	4.26 (.79)	4.02 (.78)	**4.46 (.74)**	−9.271(969.718), .000
• I teach why a lesson or task or experience is important	4.24 (.69)	**4.32 (.65)**	4.18 (.71)	3.235(1018), .001
• I point out to my students the consequences of their decisions and actions	4.28 (.65)	**4.43 (.59)**	4.16 (.68)	6.682(1018), .000

Bold refers to the highest means and illustrates differences between Finnish and Iranian teachers.

Results

Overall, teachers in both countries rated their competence to teach purpose high (Table 2). Still, t-tests showed that Iranian teachers' ($M_{\text{Iranian}} = 4.31$; SD = .53) estimations were statistically significantly higher than those of Finnish teachers' ($M_{\text{Finnish}} = 4.15$; SD = .53) ($t(1018) = -4.859, p = .000$). Also, the means of each item were compared separately, which showed that Iranian teachers seem to concentrate more than Finnish teachers on discussion and on *reflections on purpose in life* ($t(862.513) = -11.387, p = .000$) and *teaching plans for the future* ($t(-969.718) = 9.271, p = .000$). However, Finnish teachers' evaluations showed that they *taught importance* ($t(1018) = 3.235, p = .001$) and pointed out the *consequences* of students' decisions and actions ($t(969.718) = -9.271, p = .000$) more often than Iranians.

The way in which the subject matter affected teachers' self-perception of teaching purpose was studied separately for the Iranian and Finnish cases using one-way analyses of variance. Among Iranians, there were no statistically significant differences between the teachers, as can be seen in Table 3a. In other words, all Iranian teachers evaluated their competence for teaching purpose as being high, regardless of the subject taught. In contrast, among Finnish teachers there were statistically significant relationships between the subject taught and teachers' self-perceptions in three out of four aspects of teaching purpose. First, Finnish teachers differed in their views on the *guiding purpose in life* ($F(4) = 13.01, p = .000$, $\eta_p^2 = .13$). Tukey's pairwise comparisons showed that teachers of religious education scored statistically significantly higher than all other teachers, including class teachers ($p = .000$; $M = 3.78$, SD = .89) and teachers of science ($p = .000$; $M = 3.38$, SD = .86), social science ($p = .014$; $M = 3.97$, SD = .87) and languages ($p = .000$; $M = 3.80$, SD = .86). Further, it should be noted that science teachers scored statistically significantly lower than class teachers ($p = .012$), social science teachers ($p = .009$) and language teachers ($p = .04$). Second, *teaching planfulness* also varied ($F(4) = 3.600, p = .007, \eta_p^2 = .04$), and Tukey's pairwise comparisons revealed that the only statistically significant difference ($p = .009$) was between teachers of religious education ($M = 4.26$, SD = .50) and science ($M = 3.75$, SD = .71). These results indicated that, in the view of Finnish teachers, science and religious education provided the most distinct perspectives for *guiding purpose in life* and *teaching planfulness*, which in turn were the aspects most strongly emphasised by the Iranian teachers. Third, Finnish teachers showed dissimilarity in *teaching consequences* ($F(4) = 8.378, p = .000, \eta_p^2 = .09$). Games-Howell pairwise comparisons revealed that class teachers who scored highest

EDUCATION FOR PURPOSEFUL TEACHING AROUND THE WORLD

Table 3a. Iranian class teachers' and subject teachers' views of their competence to teach purpose.

Aspects of teaching purpose	Iranian teachers' subjects	M	SD	$F(4)$	p	η_p^2
Guiding purpose in life	Primary school class teachers	4.42	.710	.414	.798	.004
	Science	4.43	.638			
	Social sciences	4.53	.683			
	Language	4.45	.706			
	Religion	4.41	.773			
	Total ($n = 446$)	4.45	.697			
Teaching power distance	Primary school class teachers	4.56	.700	1.071	.371	.010
	Science	4.45	.670			
	Social sciences	4.49	.766			
	Language	4.39	.699			
	Religion	4.36	.857			
	Total ($n = 446$)	4.47	.733			
Teaching importance	Primary school class teachers	4.19	.769	.027	.999	.000
	Science	4.19	.659			
	Social sciences	4.20	.753			
	Language	4.17	.714			
	Religion	4.17	.663			
	Total ($n = 446$)	4.19	.715			
Teaching consequences	Primary school class teachers	4.19	.726	.366	.833	.003
	Science	4.22	.626			
	Social sciences	4.12	.730			
	Language	4.14	.677			
	Religion	4.13	.684			
	Total ($n = 446$)	4.17	.690			

($M = 4.60$, SD $= .50$) differed statistically significantly from teachers of science ($p = .000$; $M = 4.22$, SD $= .49$), social science ($p = .010$; $M = 4.26$, SD $= .51$) and languages ($p = .009$; $M = 4.27$, SD $= .72$) in teaching consequences, but not from teachers of religious education ($p = .249$; $M = 4.39$, SD $= .55$). Fourth, as regards *teaching importance*, Finnish teachers of various subjects did not differ from one another ($F(4) = 1.598, p = .174, \eta_p^2 = .017$) (Table 3b).

Next, whether ethical sensitivity predicted teaching purpose was studied by performing linear regression analyses using the Enter method for Iranian and Finnish samples separately. As shown in Tables 4a and 4b, ethical sensitivity predicted both Iranian and Finnish teachers' competence to teach purpose: *guiding purpose in life* ($F_{Iranian}(4) = 12.183, p = .000, \Delta R^2 = .075$; $F_{Finnish}(4) = 10.041, p = .000, \Delta R^2 = .072$), *teaching planfulness* ($F_{Iranian}(4) = 11.736, p = .000, \Delta R^2 = .067$; $F_{Finnish}(4) = 11.736, p = .000, \Delta R^2 = .085$), *teaching importance* ($F_{Iranian}(4) = 7.945, p = .000, \Delta R^2 = .048$; $F_{Finnish}(4) = 10.617, p = .000, \Delta R^2 = .077$) and *teaching consequences* ($F_{Iranian}(4) = 11.602, p = .000, \Delta R^2 = .020$; $F_{Finnish}(4) = 11.602, p = .000, \Delta R^2 = .084$). However, the most influential dimensions of ethical sensitivity were CCO among the Iranians and REI among the Finns, since these dimensions predicted all four elements of purpose teaching. However, the predictive power of the regression models was modest.

Discussion

This study examined Finnish and Iranian teachers' views of their competence to teach 'purpose'. The results showed that in both countries teachers estimated their competence as high, with Iranian teachers estimating their competence higher than their Finnish colleagues. In supporting students' formation of purpose, Iranian and Finnish teachers emphasised different strategies. Iranian teachers seem to guide their students explicitly to finding purpose in life and planning their future. These aspects were emphasised regardless of the subject

EDUCATION FOR PURPOSEFUL TEACHING AROUND THE WORLD

Table 3b. Finnish class teachers' and subject teachers' views of their competence to teach purpose.

Aspects of teaching purpose	Finnish teachers' subjects	M	SD	F(4)	p	η_p^2
Guiding purpose in life	Primary school class teachers	3.78	.890	13.006	.000	.126
	Science	3.38	.864			
	Social sciences	3.97	.870			
	Language	3.80	.858			
	Religion	4.61	.495			
	Total (n = 366)	3.81	.900			
Teaching planfulness	Primary school class teachers	3.92	.794	3.600	.007	.038
	Science	3.75	.713			
	Social sciences	4.18	.626			
	Language	3.98	.845			
	Religion	4.26	.554			
	Total (n = 366)	3.96	.765			
Teaching importance	Primary school class teachers	4.38	.598	1.598	.174	.017
	Science	4.19	.614			
	Social sciences	4.24	.606			
	Language	4.22	.786			
	Religion	4.37	.589			
	Total (n = 366)	4.30	.640			
Teaching consequences	Primary school class teachers	4.60	.504	8.378	.000	.085
	Science	4.22	.487			
	Social sciences	4.26	.511			
	Language	4.27	.718			
	Religion	4.39	.547			
	Total (n = 366)	4.42	.571			

Table 4a. Summary of regression analysis for Iranian teachers.

	Purpose		Planfulness		Importance		Consequences	
Predictor	B	β	B	β	B	β	B	β
TPO	−.041	−.036	.028	.023	−.066	−.057	−.023	−.021
CCO	.259***	.196	.256***	.184	.239***	.179	.161*	.127
REI	.089	.064	.136*	.069	.097	.069	.059	.045
ICAO	.117	.064	.052	.040	.059	.065	.039	.033
n	556	–	556	–	556	–	556	–
ΔR²	.075	–	.067	–	.048	–	.020	–

***p = .000, *p < .05.

Table 4b. Summary of regression analysis for Finnish teachers.

	Purpose		Planfulness		Importance		Consequences	
Predictor	B	β	B	β	B	β	B	β
TPO	−.112	−.060	−.076	−.048	.146*	.111	.014	.011
CCO	.123	.109	.124	.073	.099	.070	.164*	.125
REI	.338***	.207	.304***	.219	.152**	.131	.142**	.134
ICAO	.206	.110	.182*	.114	.131	.099	.163*	.133
n	464	–	464	–	464	–	464	–
ΔR²	.072	–	.085	–	.077	–	.084	–

***p = .000, **p < .01, *p < .05.

taught. In contrast, Finnish teachers tend to concentrate on explaining the importance of the tasks and on the consequences of students' actions, a result that is in line with the Finnish students' perceptions (Bundick and Tirri 2014). However, according to Finnish teachers, religious education seemed to provide a subject in which teachers can guide students to consider explicitly their purpose in life and plans for the future (Niemi 1987; Ubani 2013). Thus, the results indicate that straightforward discussions of purpose in life seem to be associated with religions and worldviews, which is natural, considering the existential nature of the purpose concept (Damon, Menon, and Bronk 2003; Frankl 1988). In Finland, this means that religion education classes offer crucially important spaces for reflections on purpose (Ubani 2013). The results also seemed to point to the fact that Finnish teacher education programmes, even multicultural ones, ignore the responsibility of addressing and educating teachers to recognise and discuss religions and worldviews (Riitaoja and Dervin 2014; Riitaoja, Poulter, and Kuusisto 2010), whereas in Iran, religion is integrated into all instruction, regardless of the subject or educational level (Hedayati et al. 2016). This might explain why competence for teaching purpose was evaluated as equally high among all Iranian teachers. However, in Iran the question remains of whether the school system provides support for the development of purpose in youth who represent ideological or religious minorities, given that teachers are required to educate students based on Islamic beliefs (Hedayati et al. 2016). For example, one of the main textbooks integrated into the Iranian curriculum has been 'religion and life', which tries to send the following message to all students, namely that the main route to finding a good life is embedded in Islamic values (e.g. Etesami 2015; TFFTES 2012, part 5 Curriculum). This hegemonic trend in the national curriculum also presents a challenge to academic freedom, as this kind of 'religious and cultural reproduction' hinders teachers and students from introducing different discourses into the classroom. Thus, teacher education programmes in both Iran and Finland are challenged to support recognition of religions and worldviews of the majorities as well as the minorities in order to support each student's holistic growth in an ethically sustainable manner.

The present study also showed that both Iranian and Finnish teachers' ethical sensitivities were associated with their competence for teaching purpose; all four elements of purpose teaching were predicted by *caring about others* in Iran and by REI in Finland. Thus, improving teachers' ethical sensitivity skills in teacher education programmes could provide a significant path for supporting teachers' competence in teaching purpose. Furthermore, regardless of different contextual insights in both Iran and Finland, one of the main applications of the present study is to integrate teaching purpose into teacher education programmes as well as into teacher professional development. Today, students and teachers are dealing with new information, knowledge, philosophies and social and cultural values with the help of information and communication technology. Teachers and students are engaged in a kind of 'selection crisis', meaning they must determine the kinds of values, knowledge and philosophy to consider in order to find their paths in their academic and personal lives. Thus, one of the main ethical and professional responsibilities of teachers and teacher educators is to help students and young people navigate and find their purpose in school communities and in society (Damon 2008). However, according to Finnish teachers, science and mathematics especially seemed to offer the most challenging contexts for teaching purpose; the teachers of these subjects felt the least competent to address purpose-related issues in their classes. Similar trends regarding maths and science teachers have been found among Finnish student teachers (Tirri and Kuusisto Forthcoming) as well as in a study on Finnish teachers' ethical sensitivity (Kuusisto, Tirri, and Rissanen 2012). The results could reflect a Western pedagogical culture in which maths and science teachers concentrate on teaching the 'pure' content of their subjects, while the integration of the subject into a moral and holistic education is seen as problematic (Grossman and Stodolsky 1995; van Veen et al. 2001). Hence, the results challenge Finnish in-service and pre-service teacher education programmes to

EDUCATION FOR PURPOSEFUL TEACHING AROUND THE WORLD

create new approaches and new cultures for mathematics and science education, which intentionally take into account the moral aspects of teaching.

To conclude, the results give an overview of the perceptions of teachers in two countries, Finland and Iran, of their competence to teach purpose. Teachers in both countries evaluated their skills as being high, but more detailed analysis showed that in Iran, teachers give instruction in purpose more directly than their colleagues in Finland, approaches that in turn reflect educational and cultural values in the respective countries. This study had a quantitative approach to teachers' self-evaluations and thus does not reveal how teachers actually teach purpose in classroom interaction nor can it explain teachers' pedagogical thinking regarding values and educational aims. More studies with observational and interview data are needed to build pedagogies and instructional approaches to teaching purpose in Finland, Iran and other countries.

Disclosure statement

No potential conflict of interest was reported by the authors.

References

Basic Education Act 628/1998. Accessed September 28, 2015. http://www.finlex.fi/en/laki/kaannokset/1998/en19980628.pdf

Benson, P. L. 2006. *All Kids Are Our Kids: What Communities Must Do to Raise Caring and Responsible Children and Adolescents*. 2nd ed. San Francisco, CA: Jossey-Bass.

Bronk, K. C. 2014. *Purpose in Life. A Critical Component of Optimal Youth Development*. Dordrecht: Springer.

Bundick, M. J. 2011. "The Benefits on Reflecting on and Discussing Purpose in Life in Emerging Adulthood." *New Directions for Youth Development* 2011 (132): 89–104. doi:10.1002/yd.430.

Bundick, M., and K. Tirri. 2014. "Teacher Support and Competencies for Fostering Youth Purpose and Psychological Well-being: Perspectives from Two Countries." *Applied Developmental Science* 18 (3): 148–162. doi:10.1080/10888691.2014.924357.

Cheng, K. K. Y., and A. B. Beigi. 2012. "Education and Religion in Iran: The Inclusiveness of EFL (English as a Foreign Language) Textbooks." *International Journal of Educational Development* 32 (2): 310–315. doi:10.1016/j.ijedudev.2011.05.006.

Damon, W. 2008. *The Path to Purpose*. New York: Free Press.

Damon, W. 2009. "The Why Question: Teachers Can Instil a Sense of Purpose." *Education Next* 9 (3): 84. Accessed September 28, 2015. http://educationnext.org/the-why-question-2/#

Damon, W., J. M. Menon, and K. C. Bronk. 2003. "The Development of Purpose During Adolescence." *Applied Developmental Science* 7 (3): 119–128. doi:10.1207/S1532480XADS0703_2.

Etesami, M. M. 2015. قران و تعلیمان دینی: دین وزندگی [Quran and Religious Education 2: Religion and Life]. Tehran: Corporation for Publication of Iranian Curricula Textbooks (in Persian).

Finnish National Board of Education. 2006. *Perusopetuksen muiden uskontojen opetussuunnitelmien perusteet 2006* [Core Curriculum for Other Religions in Basic Education]. Accessed September 28, 2015. http://www02.oph.fi/ops/perusopetus/netpkuskontojenopsit06.pdf (in Finnish).

Finnish National Board of Education. 2013. *Omana äidinkielenä opetut kielet ja opetukseen osallistuneiden määrät vuonna 2013* [Statistics of Taught Mother Tongues and Participating Students 2013]. Accessed September 28, 2015. http://www.oph.fi/download/167421_Omana_aidinkielena_opetetut_kielet_ja_opetukseen_osallistuneiden_maarat_vuon.pdf (in Finnish).

Frankl, V. E. 1988. *Man's Search for Meaning*. New York: Pocket Books.

Gholami, K., E. Kuusisto, and K. Tirri. 2015. "Is Ethical Sensitivity in Teaching Culturally Bound? Comparing Finnish and Iranian Teachers' Ethical Sensitivity." *Compare: A Journal of Comparative and International Education* 45 (6): 886–907. doi:10.1080/03057925.2014.984588.

Gholami, K., and K. Tirri. 2012. "The Cultural Dependence of the Ethical Sensitivity Scale Questionnaire: The Case of Iranian Kurdish Teachers." *Education Research International* 2012: 1–8. doi:10.1155/2012/387027.

Goals and Tasks of Supreme Council of Cultural Revolution. 1985. Accessed October 15, 2015. http:// ms.farhangoelm.ir/legislation-Bank/ههداف-و-وظایف-شورای-عالی-انقلاب-فرهنگی (in Persian).

Grossman, P. L., and S. S. Stodolsky. 1995. "Content as Context: The Role of School Subjects in Secondary School Teaching." *Educational Researcher* 24 (8): 5–11, 23.

Hedayati, N., E. Kuusisto, K. Gholami, and K. Tirri. 2016. "Values and Worldviews of Iranian Teacher Education". Manuscript, University of Helsinki.

Hofstede, G., G. J. Hofstede, and M. Minkov. 2010. *Cultures and Organizations: Software of the Mind*. 3rd ed. New York, NY: McGraw Hill.

Holm, G., and M. Londen. 2010. "The Discourse on Multicultural Education in Finland: Education for Whom?" *Intercultural Education* 21 (2): 107–120. doi:10.1080/14675981003696222.

Hopmann, S. 2007. "Restrained Teaching: The Common Core of Didaktik." *European Educational Research Journal* 6 (2): 109–124. doi:10.2304/eerj.2007.6.2.109.

Kansanen, P., and M. Meri. 1999. "The Didactic Relation in the Teaching-Studying-Learning-Process." *The TNTEE Journal* 2 (1): 107–116.

Kansanen, P., K. Tirri, M. Meri, L. Krokfors, J. Husu, and R. Jyrhämä. 2000. *Teachers' Pedagogical Thinking: Theoretical Landscapes, Practical Challenges*. New York: Peter Lang.

Kheiltash, O., and V. D. Rust. 2009. "Inequalities in Iranian Education: Representations of Gender, Socioeconomic Status, Ethnic Diversity, and Religious Diversity in School Textbooks and Curricula." In *Inequality in Education: Comparative and International Perspectives*, edited by D. B. Holsinger and W. J. Jacob, 392–416. Hong Kong: Springer.

Koshy, S., and J. M. Mariano. 2011. "Promoting Youth Purpose: A Review of the literature." *New Directions for Youth Development* 2011 (132): 13–29.

Kumpulainen, T., (ed). 2015. *Key Figures on Early Childhood and Basic Education in Finland*. Finnish National Board of Education. Accessed September 28. http://www.oph.fi/download/170048_key_figures_on_early_childhood_and_basic_education_in_finland.pdf

Kuusisto, E., K. Gholami, I. W. Schütte, M. V. C. Wolfensberger, and K. Tirri. Forthcoming. "Culturally-bound Elements of Ethical Sensitivity: Multiple Case Studies from the Netherlands, Finland, and Iran." In *Handbook on Comparative and International Studies in Education*, edited by D. Sharpes. Charlotte, NC: Information Age Publishing.

Kuusisto, E., K. Tirri, and I. Rissanen. 2012. "Finnish Teachers' Ethical Sensitivity." *Education Research International* 2012: 1–10. doi:10.1155/2012/351879.

Malin, H., T. S. Reilly, B. Quinn, and S. Moran. 2014. "Adolescent Purpose Development: Exploring Empathy, Discovering Roles, Shifting Priorities, and Creating Pathways." *Journal of Research on Adolescence* 24 (1): 186–199. doi:10.1111/jora.12051.

Mariano, J. M. 2014. "Introduction to Special Section: Understanding Paths to Youth Purpose – Why Content and Contexts Matter." *Applied Developmental Science* 18 (3): 139–147. doi:10.1080/10888 691.2014.924356.

Mariano, J. M., J. Going, K. Schrock, and K. Sweeting. 2011. "Youth Purpose and The Perception Of Social Supports Among African-American Girls." *Journal of Youth Studies* 14 (8): 921–937. doi:10.1080/13 676261.2011.609537.

Mehran, G. 2003. "Khatami, Political Reform and Education in Iran." *Comparative Education* 39 (3): 311–329. doi:10.1080/0305006032000134391.

Molaiinejad, A., and A. Zakavati. 2008. "Comparison of Teacher Education Curriculum in Iran, France, Malaysia, Japan, and England." *Educational Innovation Quarterly* 26 (7): 35–62 (in Persian).

Moran, S. 2009. "Purpose: Giftedness in Intrapersonal Intelligence." *High Ability Studies* 20 (2): 143–159.

National Core Curriculum for Basic Education. 2014. Helsinki: Finnish National Board of Education. Accessed September 28, 2015. http://www.oph.fi/download/163777_perusopetuksen_opetussuunnitelman_perusteet_2014.pdf (in Finnish).

Niemi, H. 1987. *The Meaning of Life Among Secondary School Pupils. A Theoretical Framework and Some Initial Results*. Research Bulletin 65. Helsinki: Department of Education. University of Helsinki.

Niemi, H. 2012. "The Societal Factors Contributing to Education and Schooling in Finland." In *Miracle of Education*, edited by H. Niemi, A. Toom, and A. Kallioniemi, 19–38. Rotterdam: Sense Publishers.

Nurmi, J.-E. 1991. "How do Adolescents See their Future? A Review of the Development of Future Orientation and Planning." *Developmental Review* 11: 1–59.

Paivandi, S. 2012. "The Meaning of The Islamization of the School in Iran." In *Education in West Asia*, edited by M. Ahmed, 79–102. London: Bloomsbury.

Poulter, S. 2013. *Kansalaisena maailmassa: Koulun uskonnonopetuksen yhteiskunnallisen tehtävän tarkastelua* [Citizenship in a Secular Age. Finnish Religious Education as a Place of Civic Education]. Tampere: Yliopistopaino (in Finnish.)

Riitaoja, A.-L., and F. Dervin. 2014. "Interreligious Dialogue in Schools: Beyond Asymmetry and Categorisation?" *Language and Intercultural Communication* 14 (1): 76–90. doi:10.1080/14708477 .2013.866125.

Riitaoja, A.-L., S. Poulter, and A. Kuusisto. 2010. "Worldviews and Multicultural Education in the Finnish Context – A Critical Philosophical Approach to Theory and Practices." *Finnish Journal of Ethnicity and Migration* 5 (3): 87–95.

Soltan Zadeh, M. 2012. "History Education and the Construction of National Identity in Iran." FIU Electronic theses and dissertations. Paper 601. Accessed September 28, 2015. http://digitalcommons. fiu.edu/etd/601

Teacher's Professional Ethics and Ethical Principles. 2010. Helsinki: Trade Union of Education in Finland OAJ.

TFFTES. 2012. *The Theoretical Foundation of Fundamental Transformation in the Educational System of the Islamic Republic of Iran.* Accessed October 5, 2015. http://www.medu.ir/ (in Persian).

Tirri, K. 2011. "Holistic School Pedagogy and Values: Finnish Teachers' and Students' Perspectives." *International Journal of Educational Research* 50 (2): 159–165. doi:10.1016/j.ijer.2011.07.010.

Tirri, K. 2012. "The Core of School Pedagogy: Finnish Teachers' Views of the Educational Purposefulness of Their Teaching." In *Miracle of Education*, edited by H. Niemi. A. Toom, and A. Kallioniemi, 55–66. Rotterdam: Sense Publishers.

Tirri, K. 2014. "The Last 40 Years in Finnish Teacher Education." *Journal of Education for Teaching* 40 (5): 600–609. doi:10.1080/02607476.2014.956545.

Tirri, K., and E. Kuusisto. Forthcoming. "How Can Purpose Be Taught?" *Journal of Religious Education*.

Tirri, K., and E. Kuusisto. 2013. "How Finland Serves Gifted and Talented Pupils." *Journal for the Education of the Gifted* 36 (1): 84–96.

Tirri, K., and P. Nokelainen. 2011. *Measuring Multiple Intelligences and Moral Sensitivities in Education.* Rotterdam: Sense Publishers.

Ubani, M. 2013. "Existentially Sensitive Education." In *The Routledge International Handbook of Education, Religion and Values*, edited by J. Athur and T. Lovat, 42–54. Abingdon: Routledge.

Uljens, M., and C. Nyman. 2013. "Educational Leadership in Finland or Building a Nation with Bildung." In *Transnational Influence on Values and Practices in Nordic Educational Leadership: Is There a Nordic Model?*, edited by L. Moos, 31–48. Dordrecht: Springer. doi: 10.1007/978-94-007-6226-8_3.

van Veen, K., P. Sleegers, T. Bergen, and C. Klaassen. 2001. "Professional Orientations of Secondary School Teachers Towards Their Work." *Teaching and Teacher Education* 17 (2): 175–194. doi:10.1016/ S0742-051X(00)00050-0.

Principles and methods to guide education for purpose: a Brazilian experience

Ulisses F. Araujo ⓘ, Valeria Amorim Arantes ⓘ, Hanna Cebel Danza,
Viviane Potenza Guimarães Pinheiro and Monica Garbin

ABSTRACT

This article presents a Brazilian experience in training teachers to educate for purpose. Understanding that purpose is a value to be constructed through real-world and contextualised experiences, the authors discuss some psychological processes that underlie purpose development. Then the authors show how these processes are used in a purpose development programme they have conducted for in-service and pre-service teachers over the past six years. Using innovative pedagogies, such as Problem-Based Learning, Project-Based Learning, and Design Thinking, the authors describe the steps that teachers have to follow in project development, examples of the results accomplished with this kind of programme, and research findings that are being conducted to analyse the principles and results of this approach for training teachers in how to educate youth for purpose.

Introduction

Training teachers to foster purpose development among the new generation of students is a goal around the world. Education is not only for transmitting knowledge but also for changing the mindset of students and the whole community. This paper shares the authors' experiences to foster purpose through an educational approach in which teachers, as well as students, learn by doing. These active learning methods and psychological processes support teacher effectiveness in introducing meaningful classroom practices to accomplish purpose development.

Education for purpose

Purpose is essential to move individuals to accomplish something that is both important to the self and directed at making a difference in the world beyond the self (Damon and Colby 2015; Damon, Menon, and Bronk 2003). Purpose is an internal representation of oneself that integrates four dimensions: personal meaning, intention, engagement and the effect the person has on others. Purpose is related to identity development (Bronk 2011) and the future directedness of actions, achievements, persistence and motivation to act in accordance with the purpose (Bundick 2011). Purpose organises a coherent vision of a student's future that helps the individual view everyday activities, like schoolwork, in meaningful, relevant, motivated ways (Koshy and Mariano 2011).

Education can play an essential role in purpose development by leading youth to construct identity and future goals (Bundick and Tirri 2014; Damon 2008). School activities can expose students to caring adults who can guide them towards meaningful and prosocial ways to engage their personal interests (Damon 2009). Furthermore, school can help youth contemplate awareness, appreciation, and expression of both positive and negative emotions. Educational interventions that aim to construct values, interpersonal relationships, dialogue and self-knowledge can be helpful for developing life purpose in students (Martínez 2001; Puig 1995, 2007; Puig and Martín 2010).

Educational interventions to develop purpose should be based on principles of uncertainty and complexity because human development is a probabilistic, not a deterministic, phenomenon (Araujo, Puig, and Arantes 2007; Morin 1990). Schools interested in purposeful education should search for strategies that increase the probability that the beyond-the-self impact of students' actions is made visible to students. Such visibility helps these impacts integrate into the student's own psychological projections of themselves, increasing the possibility that purpose becomes a central value for them. Furthermore, fostering purpose development in schools not only helps students grow in their self-representation and moral identity, but also can help build 'moral atmospheres' and 'moral climates' within the school community (Araújo and Arantes 2009; Narvaez 2006; Power and Higgins-D'Alessandro 2008). Moral climates are especially helpful for developing the beyond-the-self dimension of purpose (Damon 2008).

Teachers are particularly important for these strategies because both teachers' character traits and their pedagogical skills enhance student purpose development (Bundick and Tirri 2014). Teachers' strong cognitive and verbal abilities; relevant content knowledge and pedagogical delivery skills; understanding of the cognitive, social, and emotional processes that undergird student learning; and abilities to adapt to changing circumstances enhance student academic achievement (Darling-Hammond 2000; Darling-Hammond and Bransford 2005; Rice 2003). They also help students' future orientation and planning, consideration of the consequences of their actions, reflective capacities and empathic capabilities, and connection of their school learning to what is important in their lives (Bundick and Tirri 2014; Damon 2009).

Teachers can help students develop self-knowledge about their values and feelings by giving students contextualised situations in which to construct purpose based on students' moral identities. Teachers act as tutors, strengthening the autonomy of students to make plans about their futures. These plans, in turn, develop further as students work through problems presented by the situations (Araujo et al. 2014; Decker and Bouhuijs 2009). Teachers' roles move from someone responsible for transmitting knowledge to students to someone mediating student participation in activities of consequence through active, interactive, collaborative teaching methods (Araujo et al. 2014; Decker and Bouhuijs 2009; Shulman 2004; Weimer 2002).

According to Araújo (2012, 393): 'education can be an intellectual adventure, mediated by teachers who allow students a voice, promote collective and cooperative learning experiences, encourage curiosity and give them conditions to find answers to their own questions about everyday life and scientific knowledge'. As a result, teachers develop close relationships with students and serve as mediators between students' growing purposes and the world so they can open new possibilities to the students (Decker and Bouhuijs 2009; Rué 2009).

Purpose based on values

Purpose can be considered a strongly *valued*, central part of an individual's identity, especially the moral part of identity that aims to impact the world beyond the self. Central, stable values are building blocks of different types of purposes. Educating for purpose, therefore, is strengthened when teachers focus on making students more intentional regarding which values are central to their self-representations.

That brings to the fore the question: What are values, and how are values constructed psychologically? Piaget (1954) suggested that values are constructed from affective assessments of individuals' own experiences and from affective projections onto objects or other people. Values originate from a dynamic psychological regulatory system between the person and the external world. This regulation between the individual and the environment occurs through the continued interaction of personal values and social rules. Over time, this interaction develops a value-*specific* system separate from the original, general psychological system, and the values system becomes wider in scope and more stable. More stable values, in turn, lead individuals to set standards for their own behaviour, which becomes organised into behavioural norms that influence the person to act accordingly (Piaget and Gréco [1959] 1974). These self-developed, self-regulating behavioural norms are the foundation of purpose.

In the 1990s, this view of values as a dynamic system became relevant in moral psychology as scholars sought to understand the relationship between moral thoughts and actions. For example, Blasi (1995) indicated that, upon values' integration into emotional systems, values provide a basis for the construction of identity by improving the consistency between moral motivations and moral actions through progressive degrees of integration. As a result, an isolated value is less powerful in influencing thinking and behaviour, whereas a more integrated value is central to a person's identity and cognition. As values become more integrated, moral feelings such as guilt, sadness, remorse, anger and shame arise (Araujo 2000, 2003; Lewis, Haviland-Jones, and Barrett 2010; Muris and Meesters 2014; Pinheiro 2009; Pinheiro and Arantes 2015). Adding this moral tone to self-defined behavioural norms becomes a beyond-the-self-focused purpose.

The scholarly literature is not clear about how elements of purpose and morality cohere. Some scholars, such as Damon (1995), believe that one's moral values are central to one's *self-concept* starting in childhood and, therefore, are foundational to purpose development. But other scholars, such as La Taille (1996), suggest moral values are tied to *personal identity*, and differences in moral behaviour between individuals reflect differences in the moral values each holds.

Interpreting Piaget's ideas and addressing this disagreement between self-concept and personal identity, values belong to the affective dimension of the human psyche (Araujo, Puig, and Arantes 2007). Values are constructed based on individuals' actions and projections on to the objective and subjective world (Araujo, Puig, and Arantes 2007). As values are constructed, they affect self-representations, which can become integrated into a system that 'sifts' values as more central or more peripheral in importance. What determines this 'positioning' in a person's identity is the intensity of the emotional 'charge' linked to a specific value. Central values are associated with more intense feelings (Araujo, Puig, and Arantes 2007).

As a stable conception of the future within the person's identity, purpose reinforces itself through positive feelings when events go well and through resilience when events are difficult (Moran 2015). Purpose develops as meaningful opportunities to engage other people are discovered, fostered, pursued, and concretised with the support and guidance of teachers, friends, family and caring adults from a variety of life domains (Moran et al. 2012). Educational experiences with a higher likelihood of giving students such emotional charges are more likely to influence their values and, thus, their purposes.

Innovative pedagogies to develop youth purpose

Problem-Based Learning, Project-Based Learning and Design Thinking can help individuals actively construct their life purposes. These learning methodologies bring coherence to values, goals and meanings important to the person. They help individuals integrate their experiences into a personal beacon for their futures by emphasising the needs, possibilities, and opportunities for individuals and communities (Araújo 2012; Araujo and Arantes 2014; Araujo et al. 2014).

These active-learning approaches have become implemented more often at all educational levels around the world (Araujo and Arantes 2014). First, Problem-Based Learning is a pedagogical strategy for posing significant, contextualised, real-world situations, and providing resources, guidance, and instruction to students as they develop content knowledge and problem-solving skills (Mayo et al. 1993). Second, complementary to Problem-Based Learning is Project-Based Learning (De Graaff and Kolmos 2007). The word *project* comes from the Latin *projectus*, which means 'jutting out'. A project involves launching something into the world, which requires developing abilities to search for and select goals from a set of values and to anticipate actions that realise those goals (Machado 2000). Third, Design Thinking integrates multidisciplinary collaboration and iterative improvement to produce innovative products and services focused on the end-user's needs (IDEO 2009; Plattner, Meinel, and Leifer 2011).

From start to finish, these methodologies emphasise values and beyond-the-self impact because they focus not only on completing tasks but also on creating effects in the world. Solutions arise from careful study of how a designed solution affects a person or a community. The designer listens to current and potential users to understand their perspectives first, and only then creates a solution.

These three methodologies, when applied to schools, give purpose to schoolwork and to individual students. They empower students and support the development of purpose in its moral, beyond-the-self dimension. Students become immersed in real-world situations, so purpose is contextualised and not an abstract concept. Students listen to the needs, desires and necessities of others, so purpose becomes other oriented. Students search for effective ways to make the world better through creative and innovative solutions, so purpose results in prosocial effects. These educational experiences support students to take an active role in constructing purposes based on moral values.

First, students work in collaborative groups to solve problems. They collect stories from and listening to the needs of the people for whom the project aims to help. Second, student groups translate what was heard into frameworks, solutions and prototypes to improve others' well-being (Araujo and Arantes 2014; Araujo et al. 2014). Third, student groups deliver the prototypes to potential users to consider the solution's feasibility, viability and desirability.

A teacher training programme in Brazil

Over the past six years, two Brazilian universities launched programmes to direct more than 3000 undergraduate-level teacher candidates and graduate-level teachers-in-service towards values-based prosocial themes. Specific themes varied according to the specific university. For example, the University of São Paulo defined prosocial projects in relation to human rights issues included in the Universal Human Rights Declaration (1948), whereas the Virtual University of São Paulo focused on themes that promote ethics and citizenship in schools. Within these broad themes, each collaborative group of teachers-in-training defined a specific problem based on local needs and values to work on.

Incorporating Problem-Based Learning, Project-Based Learning and Design Thinking, these programmes required teachers to work collaboratively to solve problems in their school communities (Araujo and Arantes 2014). They spent approximately four weeks formulating a specific problem to investigate, approaching and listening to community members, continually clarifying and refining the problem, and seeking and mapping information about how their theme was reflected in the daily life of their schools. Then, they created the first solution prototype, showed it to the school community for discussion and feedback, then improved the prototype iteratively until the designers and the school community members felt that the solution worked well. The whole process took 15 weeks. Below are three brief examples that depict specific instances of this process and the results that ensued.

An app to help deaf students learn the periodic table

One team of science teachers aimed to develop tools to improve citizenship in education. They observed a public school in the city of Indaiatuba, eventually focusing on the challenges that deaf students faced in chemistry class. After searching for and mapping currently available tools, they realised there were no mobile apps to help deaf students learn the periodic table. So they prototyped an app that linked Brazilian Sign Language to the periodic table. These teachers realised the value of accessible information in equalising classroom situations to be more inclusive for a variety of learner types. This value drove their project's purpose to improve accessibility for one type of learner: deaf students.

A water filter for cooking

Another team of undergraduate teacher candidates decided to address water shortage issues in the local area by visiting a nearby slum to talk to residents about their water usage. Through careful observation of residents' daily lives, the teachers noticed that, although everyone had a water filter in their homes, no one used filtered water for cooking. They said it took too long to fill a pan with filtered water. So the teachers prototyped an inexpensive filter with a bigger capacity and faster water release. At the end of the project, they delivered to the community a 20-litre water filter with a big tap that cost only US$15. These teachers realised the value of convenience for maintaining individual and community health. This value drove their project's purpose to make available an inexpensive, easy-to-use tool for cooking with cleaner water.

A website for youth to learn about possible careers

A third team recognised that young people may not reflect upon their vocational strengths and abilities in order to make good career decisions. They collaborated with university first-year students and high school pupils so as better to understand how and when youth encounter or seek information about career options. Team members created a website for adolescents to explore professions. This website used more youth-friendly language and organisation. For example, the teachers divided the website into three areas based on what a particular young person might need: A 'Basic' area for youth who do not know what to do, an 'Application' area for youth seeking college applications, and a 'Job' area for youth exploring specific professional fields. This teacher team came to understand that interacting with the website, itself, was an intervention that helped young people develop their own life purposes as they navigated career information. They realised the values of exploration and individuation. These values drove their project's purpose to create an interactive platform for youth to hone their vocational interests and aptitudes that, in turn, could help those youth not only hold jobs but also find purpose.

Final remarks

Dynamic psychological systems lead to the construction of values and, in particular, moral values. Values can become purposes through positive experiences that make some values more central within an individual's identity. Since people learn by doing, teachers that create learning situations in which students can construct purpose-developing values may be particularly sought after in the coming years. Purpose values aim to affect others positively. This paper presented three powerful active-learning methodologies that can help teachers make their pedagogy more purpose oriented.

Problem-Based Learning, Project-Based Learning and Design Thinking are three methodologies that have been effective in Brazil to train teachers-in-service and teacher candidates how they can develop purposeful projects and activities in their courses, regardless of their course disciplines. The collaborative nature of these methodologies, both among the teachers and with the community, supports a moral atmosphere in their schools, which, in turn, supports teachers' construction of their own values and purposes.

Research is underway to assess further the effectiveness of these methodologies, to improve teacher education programmes, and to transfer these opportunities to other countries. In particular, these studies assess teachers' values after the programme and whether they implement purposeful education and construct moral atmospheres in their schools. Furthermore, these studies examine whether their students construct beyond-the-self purposes after participating in active-learning projects. It may take some time to improve education to foster a purposeful citizenship and a more just society. But outcomes from these active-learning methodologies provide preliminary evidence that a collaborative values-in-interaction approach to education may speed the development of purpose-focused education.

Disclosure statement

No potential conflict of interest was reported by the authors.

ORCiD

Ulisses F. Araujo ⓘ http://orcid.org/0000-0002-2955-8281
Valeria Amorim Arantes ⓘ http://orcid.org/0000-0002-2154-6147

References

Araujo, U. F. 2000. "Escola, democracia e a construção de personalidades morais [School, Democracy and the Construction of Moral Personalities]." *Educação e Pesquisa* [Education and Research] 26 (2): 91–107.

Araujo, U. F. 2012. "Promoting Ethical and Environmental Awareness in Vulnerable Communities: A Research Action Plan." *Journal of Moral Education* 41: 389–397.

Araujo, U. F., and V. A. Arantes. 2009. "The Ethics and Citizenship Programme: A Brazilian Experience in Moral Education." *Journal of Moral Education* 38: 489–511.

Araujo, U. F., and V. A. Arantes. 2014. "Re-inventing School to Develop Active Citizens." In *Positive Psychology in Latin America, Cross-cultural. Advancements in Positive Psychology*. 10 vol, edited by A. Castro Solano, 241–254. New York: Springer.

Araujo, U. F., R. Fruchter, M. C. Garbin, L. N. Pascoalino, and V. A. Arantes. 2014. "The Reorganization of Time, Space, and Relationships in School with the Use of Active Learning Methodologies and Collaborative Tools." *Educação temática digital, supl. pesquisa, desenvolvimento e formação na educação* [In Digital Thematic Education, suppl. Research, Development and Training in Education] 16 (1): 84–89.

Araujo, U. F., J. M. Puig, and V. A. Arantes. 2007. *Educação e valores: Pontos e contrapontos* [Education and Values: Points and Counterpoints]. São Paulo: Summus.

Blasi, A. 1995. "The Development of Identity: Some Implications for Moral Functioning." In *The Moral Self*, edited by G. Noam and T. Wren, 99–122. Cambridge, MA: The MIT Press.

Bronk, K. C. 2011. "The Role of Purpose in Life in Healthy Identity Formation: A Grounded Model." In *New Directions for Youth Development*, edited by Jennifer Mariano, 31–44. San Francisco, CA: Jossey-Bass.

Bundick, M. J. 2011. "The Benefits of Reflecting on and Discussing Purpose in Life in Emerging Adults." In *New Directions for Youth Development*, edited by Jennifer Mariano, 89–103. San Francisco, CA: Jossey-Bass.

Bundick, M., and K. Tirri. 2014. "Student Perceptions of Teacher Support and Competencies for Fostering Youth Purpose and Positive Youth Development: Perspectives From Two Countries." *Applied Developmental Science* 18 (3): 148–162.

Damon, W. 1995. *Greater Expectations: Overcoming the Culture of Indulgence in America's Homes and Schools*. New York: The Free Press.

Damon, W. 2008. *The Path to Purpose: Helping Our Children Find Their Calling in Life*. New York: Simon and Schuster.

Damon, W. 2009. "The Why Question: Teachers Can Instill a Sense of Purpose." *Education Next* 9 (3): 84.

Damon, W., and A. Colby. 2015. *The Power of Ideals: The Real Story of Moral Choice*. New York: Oxford.

Damon, W., J. M. Menon, and K. Bronk. 2003. "The Development of Purpose During Adolescence." *Applied Developmental Science* 7 (3): 119–128.

Darling-Hammond, L. 2000. "Teacher Quality and Student Achievement." *Education Policy Analysis Archives* 8 (1): 1–44.

Darling-Hammond, L., and J. Bransford. 2005. *Preparing Teachers for a Changing World: What Teachers Should Learn and Be Able to Do*. 1st ed. San Francisco, CA: Jossey-Bass.

Decker, I. R., and P. A. J. Bouhuijs. 2009. "Aprendizagem baseada em problemas e metodologia da problematização: Identificando e analisando continuidades e descontinuidades nos processos de ensino-aprendizagem [Problem-based Learning and Methodology of Questioning: Identifying

EDUCATION FOR PURPOSEFUL TEACHING AROUND THE WORLD

and Analyzing Continuities and Discontinuities in Teaching–Learning Processes]." In *Aprendizagem baseada em problemas no ensino superior* [Problem-based Learning in Higher Education], edited by Ulisses Araujo and Genoveva Sastre, 177–204. São Paulo: Summus.

De Graaff, E., and A. Kolmos. 2007. "History of Problem-based and Project-based Learning." In *Management of Change: Implementation of Problem-Based and Project-Based Learning in Engineering*, edited by Erik De Graaff and Anette Kolmos, 1–8. Rotterdam: Sense.

IDEO. 2009. Human-centered Design Toolkit. http://www.ideo.com/work/human-centered-design-toolkit.

Koshy, S. I., and J. M. Mariano. 2011. "Promoting Youth Purpose: A Review of the Literature." In *New Directions for Youth Development*, edited by Jennifer Mariano, 13–29. San Francisco, CA: Jossey-Bass.

La Taille, Y. D. 1996. "A indisciplina e o sentimento de vergonha [Indiscipline and Shame]." In *Indisciplina na escola: Alternativas teóricas e práticas* [Indiscipline in School: Theoretical and Practical Alternatives], edited by Julio Groppa Aquino, 9–23. São Paulo: Summus.

Lewis, M., J. M. Haviland-Jones, and L. F. Barrett. 2010. *Handbook of Emotions*. New York: Guilford Press.

Machado, N. 2000. *Educação: Projetos e valores* [Education: Projects and Values]. São Paulo: Escrituras Editora.

Martínez, M. 2001. "Escuela y construcción de valores [School and Values Development]." In *Un lugar llamado escuela: En la sociedad de la información y de la diversidad* [A Place Called School: In the Information Society and Diversity], edited by Miquel Martínez and C. Bujons, 26–48. Barcelona: Ariel.

Mayo, P., M. B. Donnelly, P. P. Nash, and R. W. Schwartz. 1993. "Student Perceptions of Tutor Effectiveness in a Problem-based Surgery Clerkship." *Teaching and Learning in Medicine* 5 (4): 227–233.

Moran, S. 2015. "Adolescent Aspirations for Change: Creativity as a Life Purpose." *Asia Pacific Education Review* 16 (2): 167–175. doi:10.1007/s12564-015-9363-z.

Moran, S., M. J. Bundick, H. Malin, and T. S. Reilly. 2012. "How Supportive of Their Specific Purposes Do Youth Believe Their Family and Friends Are?" *Journal of Adolescent Research* 28 (3): 348–377. doi:10.1177/0743558412457816.

Morin, E. 1990. *Introduction à la pensée complexe* [Introduction to Complex Thought]. Paris: ESF.

Muris, P., and C. Meesters. 2014. "Small or Big in the Eyes of the Other: On the Developmental Psychopathology of Self-conscious Emotions as Shame, Guilt, and Pride." *Clinical Child and Family Psychology Review* 17 (1): 19–40. doi:10.1007/s10567-013-0137-z.

Narvaez, D. 2006. "Integrative Ethical Education." In *Handbook of Moral Development*, edited by Melanie Killen and Judith Smetana, 703–733. Mahwah, NJ: Erlbaum.

Piaget, J. 1954. *Les relations entre l'intelligence et l'affectivité dans le développement de l'enfant* [The Relations between Intelligence and Emotions in the Development of Infants]. Paris: University of Paris-Sorbonne. http://www.fondationjeanpiaget.ch.

Piaget, J., and P. Gréco. (1959) 1974. *Aprendizagem e conhecimento* [Learning and Knowledge]. São Paulo: Freitas Bastos.

Pinheiro, V. P. G. A. 2009. "A generosidade e os sentimentos morais: Um estudo exploratório na perspectiva dos modelos organizadores do pensamento [Generosity and Moral Feelings: An Exploratory Study in the Perspective of the Organizing Models of Thought]." Master's thesis, School of Education of São Paulo University.

Pinheiro, V. P. G., and V. A. Arantes. 2015. "Values and Feelings in Young Brazilians' Purposes." *Paidéia (Ribeirão Preto)* 25 (61): 201–209.

Plattner, H., C. Meinel, and L. Leifer. 2011. *Design Thinking: Understand, Improve, Apply*. Berlin: Springer.

Power, F. C., and A. Higgins-D'Alessandro. 2008. "The Just Community Approach to Moral Education and the Moral Atmosphere of the School." In *Handbook of Moral and Character Education*, edited by Larry P. Nucci and Darcia Narvaez, 230–247. New York: Routledge.

Puig, J. M. 1995. *La educación moral en la enseñanza obligatoria* [Moral Education in the Basic Education]. Barcelona: Editorial Horsori.

Puig, J. M. 2007. "Aprender a viver [Learn to Live]." In *Educação e valores: Pontos e contrapontos* [Education and Values: Points and Counterpoints], edited by Ulisses Araujo, Josep Maria Puig, and Valéria Arantes, 65–106. São Paulo: Summus.

Puig, J. M., and X. Martín. 2010. *As sete Ccompetências básicas para educar em valores* [Seven Skills to Educate in Values]. São Paulo: Summus.

EDUCATION FOR PURPOSEFUL TEACHING AROUND THE WORLD

Rice, J. K. 2003. *Teacher Quality: Understanding the Effectiveness of Teacher Attributes*. Washington, DC: Economic Policy Institute.

Rué, J. 2009. "Aprender com autonomia no ensino superior [Learning Autonomy in Higher Education]." In *Aprendizagem baseada em problemas no ensino superior*. [Problem-based Learning in Higher Education], edited by Ulisses Araujo and Genoveva Sastre, 157–176. São Paulo: Summus.

Shulman, L. S. 2004. *The Wisdom of Practice*. San Francisco, CA: Jossey-Bass.

Weimer, M. 2002. *Learner-centered Teaching: Five Key Changes to Practice*. San Francisco, CA: Wiley.

The influence of Chinese college teachers' competence for purpose support on students' purpose development

Fei Jiang, Shan Lin and Jenni Menon Mariano

ABSTRACT

Research studies agree on the role formal education can play in facilitating students building a sense of life purpose. This paper examined the influence of Chinese college students' perceived competence of their teachers for supporting purpose on these same college students' purpose status. Portions of the Revised Youth Purpose Survey were adapted for Chinese college student and teacher populations, and then administered to 52 teachers and 213 students from a mid-size teacher training university in north-east China. There was inconsistency between teachers' self-evaluations and students' evaluations, with teachers rating themselves as more supportive of purpose than they were rated by their students. Upperclassmen reported higher levels of teacher competence for supporting purpose than lowerclassmen, and arts teachers were rated as more supportive of purpose than teachers of other subjects. Students who ranked obviously other-oriented goals as their most important purposes also rated their teachers as more competent in purpose support than students who endorsed other types of goals. Significant positive associations were found among students' ratings of teachers for purpose support and reports of purpose from students, including associations with students' purpose search and purpose identification; however, no relationship was found between students' purpose engagement and perceptions of teachers' purpose support.

Introduction

Adolescence and young adulthood are times when individuals begin to seek and explore their meaning in life (Devogler and Ebersole 1983), and to set up life goals (Massey, Gebhardt, and Garnefski 2008). Purpose is associated with many positive outcomes, and youth in higher grade levels are more likely to describe their future plans, activities to pursue those plans, and reasons that consider consequences to others as well as to themselves (Moran et al. 2013). Thus, based on educational and developmental principles, there is a growing feeling that educational institutions may have a profound role in promoting purpose among students, and that learners at progressively higher stages in their education (i.e. later adolescence and early adulthood) are important groups in which to study the impact of teacher purpose support. The feeling that institutions of learning impact purpose is shared by educators in many countries who, until only recently, have collaborated in the study of teachers' roles in purpose education. To date, only a few studies specifically examine the role of teachers and educational institutions in promoting students' purposes, but the interest is relatively widespread (i.e. around the world, such as in studies in Finland, Singapore, Brazil, the United States and other countries [for examples see: Mariano et al. 2011; Bundick and Tirri 2014]).

This paper extends the examination of teachers' roles on youths' purposes by country and by grade or age level by focusing on college instructors and their students in China. College teachers play a vital role in students' overall learning experience, and the degree to which students perceive their college instructors as being helpful influences with overall satisfaction with the college experience and strengthens a sense of purpose. A study of more than 30,000 college graduates in the United States found that students who felt they have professors who cared, who were mentors and made them excited about learning were nearly three times as likely to be thriving than those who did not feel such support; 'thriving' included a measure of 'purpose well-being' (Gallup and Purdue University 2014, 4–7). The present study however is the first, to our knowledge, to adapt measures of purpose teaching that are first used in Western countries for use among college students and teachers in mainland China.

A broad congruence between modern Chinese concepts of purpose and at least one recent purpose definition espoused by Western scholars provides a starting point for utilising Western measures of purpose for adaptation in China. In the following pages, this paper thus first highlights similarities of the Chinese view of purpose with a current Western definition. This research then discusses the extant literature on teachers' roles in students' purpose support, and outlines and reports results of this empirical study.

In order to gain a better understanding of teachers' roles in purpose education, this paper examines whether teacher competence in supporting purpose in their students matters to the purpose of those same college students with whom these teachers work. Specifically: (1) Is students' perceived teacher competence for supporting purpose consistent with teachers' self-evaluations of their own competence? (2) Are teachers' self-evaluations and students' perceived teacher competence influenced by teachers' length of teaching experience, subject of specialty, sex, students' major, student's academic achievement or by gender? (3) Does teacher competence for purpose support influence the orientation of students' life purpose (i.e. whether students endorse beyond-the-self purposes)? and (4) Does teacher competence for supporting purpose affect students' likelihood of searching for purposes, of identifying purposes, or of being actively engaged to achieve purposes?

If students' purpose growth is dependent on how supportive students think their teachers are, then an accurate perception is important for teacher professional development. This study expected Chinese college teachers to overestimate their purpose support competence compared to students' reports. The Chinese college curriculum explicitly endorses purpose instruction through extensive and compulsory courses in ideological and political education taught by specialised teachers: competence in purpose teaching is socially desirable within Chinese culture. Although teachers surveyed were not specialists in purpose instruction, the importance placed on purpose education in China should feed into teachers' desire to see and report themselves as competent in purpose support, compared to students' perceptions.

This study also expected that the longer students remain in college, the more likely they will be to rate their teachers as competent in purpose support. Remaining in college may indicate greater satisfaction with and confidence in the efficacy of the college to support the students' life goals, and upper year classmen represent retention better than their younger counterparts, who could drop out in the future due to low satisfaction with college. Perceptions of social support are related to persistence in college (Nicpon et al. 2006). Students might see their teachers' ability to support their purposes as a proxy to provide social support more generally.

Teachers' longevity in their profession should impact students' perceptions of their teachers' purpose support competence. Longer immersion in a purpose-centred culture in which purpose teaching is dominant and explicitly sanctioned should lead to greater proficiency in purpose support.

Teacher's longevity in the profession is commonly expressed through their university title, with higher ranks suggesting longer service. Although this is not always the case (i.e. an instructor may in fact have longer teaching experience, even beyond that of many associate or full-professors), this research expects that in general, this rule will hold and that teachers' rank titles will impact students' reports of teacher purpose support in a positive direction.

It is unclear however whether teachers' subject matter specialty should influence their purpose support competence as rated by students. Traditionally, arts and humanities subjects may provide more opportunity for class discussions of social issues that relate to that aspect of purpose that pertains to contributing to the world beyond the self. On the other hand, disciplines with more hands-on fieldwork (e.g. science, engineering or art) may engender more personally meaningful experiences for students that connect schoolwork to their future work. The same argument applies to the predicted effects of college major on students' experiences with their teachers: it is therefore also unclear whether students' major would impact how they rate their teachers' purpose support competence.

It is established that teacher support is important for students' growth in many ways. By extension, this research expects that students' assessment of teachers' competence of purpose support will influence students' purpose orientation (i.e. beyond-the-selfness of their purposes) as well as their purpose identification, purpose search and purpose engagement, all in a positive direction. First, Chinese purpose education is systematic, organised and curriculum-wide and the Chinese view of purpose includes cultivating the individual's aspirations as well as service to the common good. However, Chinese purpose education most strongly emphasises instruction for a common purpose, ultimately encouraging that one forfeits personal goals for the common good, and thus advocating for beyond-the-self. Thus, students who rate their teachers as supportive of purpose likely equate that competence with teaching for beyond-the-selfness. Second, it is simple logic that purpose identification and purpose engagement associate positively with teacher purpose support: students who have supportive teachers will grow in the ways in which they are supported. But in the Chinese context, this research also expects purpose search to associate positively with teacher competence because research in Eastern cultures exhibits harmony between search and achievement, whereas the opposite view is endorsed more in Western cultures (e.g. Steger et al. 2008). Studies with Chinese populations exhibit a positive relationship between purpose search and identification, proposing that the relationship of purpose search with teacher purpose support will correspond accordingly (e.g. Chan 2014).

Gender is an important variable to consider when studying ratings of social support of any kind. In general, females of college age or younger reported higher levels and different uses of social support for their goals than males (e.g. Tam and Lim 2009), even from teachers, and with only a few studies departing from this trend. It is argued that such consistent findings warrant studying males and females separately to avoid misleading conclusions and recommendations for either group. Following on this body of research, this paper expected female students to rate teachers significantly higher on purpose support competence than their male peers.

Considerable research has been conducted on whether academic variables impact positive developmental outcomes. Results are mixed, depending on the measures used (i.e. grade point average or other reports) and other factors accounted for (e.g. see approaches in multiple countries by Kirkcaldy, Furnham, and Siefen [2004]). In the current research, students' academic achievement was not a main part of the study, but assessed nonetheless considering its potential effect on students' positive perceptions of their teachers and of school. It is reasonable to suppose that students who are doing well academically will also rate their schools and teachers as effective. For this reason, this paper expected that students' academic achievement would be positively associated with their reports of teachers' purpose support competence.

The Chinese conception of purpose

In recent years, the study of purpose has gained global attention in academic research (i.e. Moran 2001; Bronk 2012; Jiang 2013; Bundick and Tirri 2014; Mariano 2014). Both Eastern and Western scholars propose scientific definitions of purpose. In China, purpose is defined as the yearning and pursuit of one's future. It is the reflection of one's worldview and standpoint (Zhang 2006). Chinese people metaphorically look on purpose as a beacon, symbolising the guiding function it provides to life. Purpose is normally classified into social purpose and personal purpose. Social purpose is the common purpose assumed to be advocated by the majority of members of a society or culture, representing this majority's hopes for what a positive society should be like; and in China, this means building the nation into a prosperous, strong, democratic and civilised modern socialist country. Personal purpose is an umbrella term referring to the multiple aspirations that individuals have, including one's desired material, spiritual and family life, one's professional goals and one's personal moral aspirations (i.e. the kind of moral character one wants to cultivate) (Jiang and Lin 2014). Purpose education in China is organised, systematic and country-wide. It is implemented with a main focus on social purpose but also with considerable attention to personal purpose (Dong 1984).

Western researchers have also defined purpose during the past decades (Baumeister 1991; Ryff and Singer 1998). For example, at the beginning of this millennium, Damon, Menon, and Bronk (2003) proposed what has now become a widely accepted definition of purpose, and one that has much congruence with common Chinese conception: 'purpose is a stable and generalised intention to accomplish something that is at once meaningful to the self and of consequence to the world beyond the self' (121). The Chinese notion and Damon, Menon, and Bronk's (2003) notion are similar in three ways. First, they both regard purpose as an intention which is directed towards the future. Purpose is an intention or an aim, and it does not only focus on the present. Purpose directs one's goal to the far-reaching future. Second, both concepts incorporate current engagement to achieve purpose (i.e. 'pursuit' in the Chinese notion and 'to accomplish something' in the Western notion). Purpose is very different from fantasy or reverie in that purpose values action rather than remaining in the realm of theory. Intentions are supposed to trigger future purposeful behaviours and guide one in the right direction to achieve one's proposed endeavours. Third, both the Chinese concept and this Western concept focus on the beyond-the-self characteristics (i.e. 'social purpose' in the Chinese notion and 'the world beyond the self' in the Western notion). Thus, future orientation, engagement and beyond-the-self aspiration constitute the major characteristics of purpose shared by Chinese and Western scholars. This congruence between Chinese and popular Western notions of purpose (i.e. Damon, Menon, and Bronk 2003) may provide an initial point of comparison for designing studies and also interpreting findings about the meaning of purpose experiences from Chinese and Western perspectives. Thus, although the current research involves a Chinese population, the Western purpose definition discussed here provides a useful backdrop for this study. Consequently, in forming hypotheses and a literature review, it was useful to draw from Chinese and Western purpose research which use the same purpose concept.

The role of the teacher in students' purpose support

A sense of purpose plays critical roles in one's development as it is linked to aspects of positive development and thriving (Ulmer, Range, and Smith 1991; Damon, Menon, and Bronk 2003; White, Wagener, and Furrow 2009; Bundick et al. 2010; Hill et al. 2010) such as overall quality of life (Ulmer, Range, and Smith 1991), life satisfaction (Cotton Bronk et al. 2009; Steger 2012) and well-being (Thauberger and Cleland 1981; Keyes, Shmotkin, and Ryff 2002; Seligman 2002), prosocial behaviour (Cotton Bronk et al. 2009; Bundick et al. 2010), happiness (French and Joseph 1999), positive affect (King et al. 2006) and coping (Reker, Peacock, and Wong 1987). Additionally, purpose in life may also exert positive influences on adolescents' school behaviours. Students who have identified a life purpose tend to be more extroverted (Pearson and Sheffield 1974), and thus may be more likely to participate in campus organisations (Doerries 1970), to enjoy planning and organising events (Yarnell 1971) and to have improved academic self-regulation pertaining to important but uninteresting or tedious learning tasks (Yeager et al. 2014).

For these reasons, studying the role of the academic context on purpose is an important area of investigation. Furthermore, there is little doubt that development is a process involving reciprocal relations and mutual constitution of self and environment over time (Lerner 1982; Markus and Kitayama 2010): so, purpose, as an important component of what makes humans flourish (Seligman 2002), does not come from nowhere. Instead, purposes are discovered, engaged and realised with the guidance and support of significant others in the environment, and school is definitely a significant component of the environment in which students are embedded. Indeed, scholars believe education should play a central role in the development of identity and future goals (Guo 2011; Wei 2015), and purpose researchers note how youth who report having a general sense of purpose also describe having social supports that enhance thriving, such as through school (Moran et al. 2013).

Additionally, social supports in the environment, such as schools, also help shape what purposes youth pursue (Grotevant 1987). In this way, teachers are important persons who serve as a vital part of a school context in which purpose emerges for young people (Bundick and Tirri 2014). Since commitment generally grows slowly but steadily in response to positive feedback, teachers could play an important role in supporting noble purposes over time by constantly providing positive feedback to students (Bronk 2012). A recent comparative study showed that in both Finland and the United States, teacher competence could help students develop purpose and students exhibited greater purpose when teachers deliberately applied some moral instruction practices among their students (Bundick and Tirri 2014). Even though people have been aware of the roles teachers could play and competencies teachers should possess to promote purpose among students, comparatively less is known about how youth purpose is supported by teachers and schools currently (Mariano et al. 2011).

In China, the role of teachers for students' moral purpose support dates back at least to the ancient Tang Dynasty (618–907 AD). In Chinese ideology, teachers' roles as moral guides have always been valued more highly than their role as academic instructors. The great Tang thinker and philosopher Yu Han proposed that teachers were those who should propagate social morality, impart professional knowledge and resolve doubts among their students (Li and Cui 2008), among which propagating the social morality ranks first in teachers' responsibilities. Yu Han's ideology on teachers' roles has since been regarded as a model for teachers in China.

Much research has been conducted among students at different educational levels to examine the function of teachers' support in students' personality and identity development as well as in their academic achievement. Teacher's support of students' emotions, support in providing materials and support of learning strategies could exert a direct positive effect on pupil's autonomous learning and efficiency (Fu and Guo 2012). Teacher's supporting activities predict students' self-esteem level and the frequency with which students tend to seek academic help from their teachers (Su and Feng 2009; Chen and Xu 2011; Du 2015). A recent study among college students indicated that student perceived teacher support affected academic emotion via self-determination, which could promote positive academic emotions and inhibit negative activities associated with academic emotions (Zhang 2012). Other research also discovered the importance of teachers' and counsellors' psychological support to students (Xue, Lin, and Zheng 2010).

During the past several decades, purpose education has gradually gained more and more attention in China. Ample research addresses characteristics of and reasoning behind college students' life purposes, as well as the guidelines, content, methods, effectiveness and risks of college purpose education (Liu 2005; Wang and Zheng 2008; Jiang and Huang 2009; Wang 2011; Wang and Song 2011; Wu 2011; Chen 2015). Youth purpose is a key component in all levels of Chinese education, and fostering a sense of life purpose is the core of the ideological and political education course (Yang, Huang, and Zhu 2010): This course is compulsory from grade one through the graduate level in the Chinese curriculum and provides the most direct and frequent opportunities for teachers to teach for purpose among students. Yet, even though the ideological and political education course provides a platform to bring purpose education into the curriculum and is a reason for students to learn and engage in purpose-related knowledge and practice, it has led purpose education down a narrow path. Purpose education is too dependent on ideological and political education teachers (Wei 2015). This course-centred approach not only neglects the greater influence that other subject teachers could exert in purpose education, but also weakens the responsibilities that teachers of other majors could take in cultivating purposeful citizens. Against this curricular backdrop, the present study is both important and timely because it can help assess the importance of Chinese students' perceptions of the capabilities of their non-purpose teaching instructors for students' positive development.

Method

Participants

Two hundred and sixty-five Chinese participants from one university in north-east China including 52 college teachers and 213 college students who were pupils of these same college teacher participants participated in the study. The data were collected in spring 2011. All participants were recruited on campus and completed a paper and pencil survey following informed consent procedures. Students were gathered on a Saturday morning in two computer labs of the school library. Guided by trained survey administrators, students spent approximately 40 minutes to complete the survey. The teachers' survey was sent to the college instructors' offices and took approximately 10 minutes to complete. No incentives were offered in the data collection process.

Instructors completing the survey (54% female) held a range of professional titles/ranks and disciplinary backgrounds: 15.4% were full-professors, 36.5% were associate professors, 40.4% were lecturers and 1.9% were assistant professors. Based on the disciplinary classification in China's college entrance examination, 42% of the teachers were science and engineering teachers, 46% were arts and humanities teachers and 12% were art teachers (i.e. music, fine art and sports-related majors). None of the instructors were ideological and political education course teachers, who are specifically trained in purpose teaching. Teachers' teaching experience was distinct as well, reflected by their years of teaching. Among the teacher sample, 20% were new teachers who had been teaching for less than five years, 38% were experienced teachers who had been teaching between 5 and 10 years and 42% were very experienced teachers who had been teaching for over 10 years.

Sixty-one per cent of the students were female, ranging from the freshman to graduate level, with 73% lower graders (freshmen and sophomores) and 27% upper graders (juniors, seniors and graduate students). Students' academic achievement was also measured in this survey by students' examination scores. Fifty percent of the students ranked among the top 25% in their class, 30% ranked in the top 26–50% of their class, 13% ranked in the lower 51–75% of their class and 4% ranked in the lowest 25% of their class. Forty-eight per cent of the students were science and engineering majors, 36% were arts and humanities majors and 16% were art majors.

Measures

This paper administered selected items from the Revised Stanford Youth Purpose Survey (Bundick et al. 2006), which were initially developed from a larger study of youth purpose in the United States (see Damon 2008a). Items from this survey have since been translated, adapted and utilised in studies in other countries including Finland and China (i.e. Bundick and Tirri 2014). Survey items were first translated into Mandarin by two Chinese scholars proficient in English who were doing research in moral and civic education, and then back-translated into English by a Chinese American who was a native Chinese speaker and who had earned a doctorate in education in the United States. The translated surveys were

EDUCATION FOR PURPOSEFUL TEACHING AROUND THE WORLD

then reviewed by another Chinese professor and piloted among Chinese college teachers and students before they were eventually applied among all the participants.

Three portions of the Revised Youth Purpose Survey (Bundick et al. 2006) were administered among the sample to examine both students' purpose status (i.e. purpose search, purpose identification, purpose engagement and purpose orientation) and students' and teachers' perceptions of teachers' competence for cultivating purpose. These three measures are described below.

Life goal ranks

In the first part of the survey, participants ranked in order of importance their first, second and third life goals from a list of 17 goals. The 17 goals were generated based on related research conducted on meaning in life and used in previous studies of youth purpose including one study in China (e.g. see Devogler and Ebersole 1980, 1981, 1983; Damon 2008b). Theoretically, a purpose in life may feature long-term intentions that are self-oriented, beyond-the-self oriented, some combination of both or simply neutral. Previous research in the United States and in China categorised the 17 life goals into these categories in this way using statistical or conceptual methods, or a combination of both (e.g. Damon 2009; Bronk and Finch 2010; Jiang and Lin 2014). Drawing from this previous work and the interpretation of the item content, the current research focused on 9 of the 17 items that have been classified as other-oriented, meaning that these items express aspiration for serving others. These items were: help others, serve God or a higher power, make the world a better place, change the way people think, create something new, make things more beautiful, discover new things about the world, support my family and friends and serve my country. The remaining eight items did not indicate obvious other-oriented intentions (i.e. the items were fulfil my duties, do the right thing and earn the respect of others) or solely reflect an interest in serving one's own material or spiritual needs (i.e. the items were make money, be successful, have fun, live life to the fullest and have a good career).

Purpose search, identification and engagement

In the second part of the survey, three subscales, with five self-report items each, assessed on a seven-point scale (1 = Strongly Disagree, 7 = Strongly Agree) participants' propensity to be seeking a purpose, to have identified a purpose or to be engaged in practices to achieve their purpose (see also Steger et al. [2006]; from which several of these items originate). Higher scores on these scales indicate higher likelihood that someone is searching for a life purpose (search, a sample item is 'I am searching for my meaning in life'), has discovered a life purpose (identification, a sample item is 'My life has a clear sense of purpose') and is engaged in specific practices towards achieving purpose in life (engagement, a sample item is 'I am always working towards accomplishing my most important goals in life'). Scales showed internal reliability (search α = .709; identification α = .804; engagement α = .649) ranging from adequate to excellent for an exploratory study (Nunnally 1978).

Teacher competence for purpose support: students' and teachers' perceptions

The third part of the survey examined perceptions of teachers' competence to cultivate purpose among students. Both students' and teachers' perceptions were gathered, with items phrased appropriately to address the student or the teacher. These items were developed from observations and interviews conducted at a group of American schools that were considered exceptional for supporting purpose in their students (i.e. as used and discussed by Andrews, Rathman, and Moran 2008; Bundick and Tirri 2014). The original list constitutes six items; however, only five were retained as the sixth item was not applicable to the specific educational context of this study in China (i.e. the removed item was, 'There are special events/days where community members come to talk about what they do'). The remaining five items, endorsed dichotomously as either true or false in this study, produced a general map of students' and teachers' respective perceptions of teacher competence for purpose at school, with a 'no' answer credited 0 and a 'yes' answer credited 1. The index of teacher competence for purpose was a sum of these five items, ranging from 0 (no perceived teacher competence for purpose support) to 5 (highest perceived teacher competence for purpose support) (total $\alpha = .714$; teacher $\alpha = .573$; student $\alpha = .719$). Teachers and students endorsed the following items as true or false with language adapted so that teachers were self-referencing and students referenced their perceptions of their teachers. Thus, teachers were asked to consider whether the statements were accurate about their own teaching, and students were asked to consider whether the statements were accurate about their teachers as a group.

Item 1: Understanding of the consequences of one's actions. This item was: 'the consequences of my decisions and actions are pointed out to me'. Purpose requires an understanding of the connection between one's efforts and actions and one's goals (Bundick and Tirri 2014, 152); this ability involves judging which actions may lead to successful fulfilment of a purpose and which may not. Furthermore, understanding consequences of one's actions involves recognition of potential benefits or harms of one's purpose for the world beyond the self (i.e. beyond-the-self purpose orientation) (Bundick and Tirri 2014, 152).

Item 2: Understanding of the importance of one's engagements. This item was: 'I am taught WHY a lesson or task or experience is important.' Students who understand how what they are doing in college is important to their lives are also more likely to see how their college coursework serves their purpose (Bundick and Tirri 2014, 153).

Item 3: Understanding of the importance of persistence towards accomplishment. This item was: 'My teachers give me opportunities to improve and resubmit my work.' Purpose involves persistence often in the face of challenge, and teachers can provide opportunities for students' improvement in schoolwork, which is particularly relevant when the student views coursework as serving their purposes.

Item 4: Understanding that one's purpose is important. This item was: 'I am expected to figure out what my purpose in life is.' The importance of cultivating one's purpose is already explicitly embedded in the Chinese college curriculum; this item assesses the perceived effectiveness of non-purpose specialist teachers in communicating this culturally endorsed value.

Item 5: Future planning. This item was: 'teachers teach me how to plan for the future'. As an ability involving prospection, the formation and pursuit of purpose suppose the ability to plan (Bundick and Tirri 2014, 152).

Background and academic achievement

Information on students' subject major, students' sex and students' grade level was collected via self-reports on the survey. Students' academic achievement was collected through their scores on the latest examination.

Analysis method

SPSS 20.0 was used in all data analysis. Independent samples t-tests were utilised to assess differences between students' and teachers' ratings of the teachers' purpose support competence, and to identify where any potential variation existed by specific survey question. A series of one-way analyses of variance (ANOVAs) then examined potential differences in students' teacher purpose support ratings by the students' purpose beyond-the-selfness orientation (i.e. via selection of first ranked life goals). ANOVAs assessed for effects on students' rating of teachers by students' grade level, subject major, sex and academic achievement, and by teacher's gender, professional position, length of teaching experience and area of teaching specialisation. Finally, correlations were run among students' perception of teacher purpose support competence and aspects of students' purpose status (i.e. purpose search, purpose identification and purpose engagement).

Results

Teachers' self-evaluations surpassed students' evaluations

As expected, independent sample t-test showed that teachers' self-evaluations on their competence for purpose support ($M = 4.56$, SD $= .85$) were significantly greater than students' evaluations of these same teachers' support ($M = 3.98$, SD $= 1.35$) ($t = 3.875$, df $= 122.535$, $p < .001$; $d = 0.51$). The efforts teachers believed they had devoted to purpose teaching were not equally perceived by their students in most cases. A series of independent sample t-tests revealed significant differences between teachers' self-evaluations and students' evaluations on four of the five items, including 'I am expected to figure out what my purpose in life is' ($t = 2.161$, df $= 114.251$, $p < .05$; $d = 0.30$; teacher $M = 0.94$, SD $= 0.235$; student $M = 0.85$, SD $= 0.353$), 'teachers teach me how to plan for the future' ($t = 3.259$, df $= 112.595$, $p < .01$; $d = 0.43$; teacher $M = 0.90$, SD $= 0.298$; Student $M = 0.74$, SD $= 0.441$), 'the consequences of my decisions and actions are pointed out to me' ($t = 3.767$, df $= 116.738$, $p < .001$; $d = 0.49$; teacher $M = 0.90$, SD $= 0.298$; student $M = 0.71$, SD $= 0.45$) and 'I am taught why a lesson or task or experience is important' ($t = 3.712$, df $= 212.000$, $p < .001$; $d = 0.35$; teacher $M = 1.00$, SD $= 0$; student $M = 0.94$, SD $= 0.24$). No significant difference was found on the item 'my teachers give me opportunities to improve and resubmit my work' (teacher $M = 0.81$, SD $= 0.39$; student $M = 0.74$, SD $= 0.44$).

Major and grade-level influence on students' perceptions of teacher competence

A series of one-way analyses of variance (ANOVAs) found effects of major and of grade level on students' perceptions of teacher competence (major $F(2, 210) = 7.717$, $p < .01$; $\eta^2 = 0.068$) grade level ($F(1, 211) = 4.650$, $p < .05$; $\eta^2 = 0.022$). Art majors had significantly higher perceptions of their teachers' competence for purpose support ($M = 4.68$, SD $= 0.66$) than science

EDUCATION FOR PURPOSEFUL TEACHING AROUND THE WORLD

Table 1. Students' first ranked life goals organised by purpose orientation.

Purpose orientation	Number of times ranked #1
Obviously other-oriented	
Help others	10
Serve God or a higher power	0
Make the world a better place	10
Change the way people think	0
Create something new	2
Make things more beautiful	0
Discover new things about the world	4
Support my family and friends	30
Serve my country	
Not obviously other-oriented	
Fulfil my duties	20
Do the right thing	10
Earn the respect of others	5
Mostly self-oriented	
Make money	3
Be successful	22
Have fun	0
Live life to the fullest	61
Have a good career	27

and engineering majors ($M = 3.94$, SD $= 1.36$; $p < .01$), and arts and humanities majors ($M = 3.69$, SD $= 1.65$; $p < .01$). There was no significant difference in perceptions between science and engineering majors and arts and humanities majors. Art majors reported the highest teacher competence for purpose support.

As expected, upper level classmen (juniors, seniors and graduate students, $M = 4.29$, SD $= 1.16$) reported greater teacher competence in purpose support than their lower grade counterparts (freshman and sophomore, $M = 3.86$, SD $= 1.38$). Possibly, the longer students stay in college, the more likely they are to glean positive experiences for their purpose from the curriculum, therefore yielding these higher reports of their teachers' competence for supporting them. No differences were found by students' gender or by academic achievement. Contrary to expectations, none of the teacher characteristics (i.e. sex, length of teaching experience, professional title or subject of specialty) were related to teachers' self-evaluations of competence.

Students' purpose is influenced by perceived teachers' purpose support

As noted, this paper specifically examined the influence of perceived teacher competence for purpose support on four important aspects of students' purpose: the beyond-the-self orientation of students' most important life purpose, and students' reports of purpose search, purpose identification and purpose engagement.

Students' beyond-the-self purpose orientation

Table 1 shows frequencies of students' first ranked life goals, which were conceptually grouped as either obviously other-oriented, not obviously other-oriented or mostly self-oriented. Thus, the beyond-the-selfness of students' purpose content was assessed via their first ranked life goals from a list of 17 possible goals (i.e. using ANOVA). As expected, students who ranked the obviously other-oriented life goals first saw their teachers as more purpose

EDUCATION FOR PURPOSEFUL TEACHING AROUND THE WORLD

Table 2. Correlations among students' ratings of teachers' purpose support and students' purpose.

	Teachers' purpose support	Purpose search	Purpose identification	Purpose engagement
Teachers' purpose support	1	0.448**	0.303**	0.035
Purpose search		1	0.179**	0.114
Purpose identification			1	0.000
Purpose engagement				1

Note: Purpose search, purpose identification and purpose engagement refer to students' self-reports.
**$p < 0.001$; $N = 213$.

supportive ($M = 4.45$, SD = 0.95) than did the students who ranked other types of life goals first (not obviously oriented life goals $M = 3.71$, SD = 1.49; Mostly self-oriented life goals $M = 3.81$, SD = 1.42) ($F(2, 210) = 5.862$, $p < .01$, $\eta^2 = 0.053$).

Students' purpose search, identification and engagement

In keeping with expectations, Table 2 shows significant positive associations between students' ratings of teacher purpose support and students' purpose search and purpose identification (effect sizes were medium; Cohen [1992, 157]); although it occurred in a positive direction, no significant relationship was found with purpose engagement.

Discussion

According to theory and previous research, promoting purpose should exert positive influence on students' school behaviours (Yeager et al. 2014) and also ultimately facilitate positive youth development (Damon, Menon, and Bronk 2003). The current study was thus designed to assess whether, and how, perceptions of college teachers' supportiveness in fact *matter* to students' purpose in life: this research especially sought to know whether this was the case within a Chinese educational context where purpose teaching is widely endorsed and officially promoted. Ultimately, understanding the role of teacher support in students' purpose in life could guide teachers' daily teaching activities, influence school policies and help structure teacher training. Results confirmed several of the expectations while revealing several nuances.

First, as expected, college teachers provided significantly higher evaluations of how competent they were in supporting their students' purpose in life than did the students themselves about their own teachers. This finding may indicate the social desirability and positivity associated with identifying oneself as an effective purpose teacher in China. However, it also indicates a possible disconnect between teachers' and students' perceptions about the efficacy of college for supporting one of the most important aspects of one's existence: one's purpose in life. A disconnect among youth and their older educators would not be unusual in any country. Such divergence seems the norm in modern society where rapid change in lifestyles and economies has led to intense transformations in people's lives even within one generation (i.e. see Giddens 1991). The finding might encourage educators in China, and elsewhere, to closely consider young people's own views of purpose and how they can be supported. Insights derived from such studies could inform teacher training. Further studies of young people's emic views may be in order and college educators should give them special attention (e.g. see Moran [2014]).

As expected, upper level classmen gave their teachers the highest ratings of purpose support competence. But the result may not necessarily indicate a general length of experience effect. Teachers' ratings of their own purpose support competence did not significantly increase by their length of experience or by their professional title, which is also an indicator of time in the profession.

Students majoring in art, however, did rate their teachers higher in purpose support competence than did their classmates with all other majors. A recent study of students with arts-related purposes may explain this. Young artists, it seems, tend to lose their sense of meaning in their artistic activity as they transition from school to work possibly more than youth pursuing other subjects (Malin 2015). Pursuing an artistic career is challenging: arts teachers in college may therefore be seen as especially important mentors and supporters by art students.

Also as expected, students' perceptions of their teachers' supportiveness did matter for their purpose in life. Students with higher teacher support ratings chose obviously other-oriented life goals as most important. According to Chinese and to some Western definitions of purpose, this choice is 'purposeful' because purpose inherently involves a beyond-the-self focus. It is surprising therefore that the same significant relationship was not found between reported teachers' support and actual purpose engagement. This could indicate a deficiency with this measure of engagement: unlike self-reports of one's inner condition of seeking and identifying purpose, engagement may be better assessed through behavioural observations and over time. Furthermore, it could be that students simply don't connect their sense of identified purpose to their actions in their lives: in-depth interviews might better capture that.

Students with higher teacher support ratings also reported greater purpose identification and search. In some other countries, purpose search would not indicate greater purpose. Yet, it is likely that in China, the harmonious relationship between identification and search is indicative of higher purpose overall, as the two variables positively correlate.

Several more findings that did not align with expectations are worth noting. Students' gender did not make a difference for their purpose support ratings. This finding does not match previous research showing gender differences in young people's reports of social support. It could be, however, that purpose support is a more specific and different type of support than the types usually assessed in such studies (i.e. instrumental support and/or emotional support), thus not yielding the same gender differences. Students' ratings of their teachers also did not show variance by academic achievement. The measure of this variable, however, was limited to examination scores. In China, such scores are common ways of assessing academic prowess; however, other achievement variables may better align with purpose.

Implications for research and for college teachers' practice in China

The findings provide a chance to look at the real situation of the implementation of teachers' role as purpose promoters in Chinese colleges. Teachers' roles as moral guides may be widely advocated in general, but may be inadequately implemented in practice (Wang and Song 2011). Purpose education is still mainly dependent on ideological and political education teachers, whereas other subject teachers' purpose teaching function is neglected (Guo 2011; Wei 2015). The reason mainly lies in the education system: first, cultivating teacher competence for purpose is not a necessary part of teacher education and teacher competence to promote purpose is not a part of teachers' evaluations. In fact, for college subject teachers, being a purpose instructor is more of a cultural tradition (Li and Cui 2008) than a real requirement. Even in *The Higher Education Law of the People's Republic of China* (1998, Chapter V Article 47), requirements on college teachers merely focus on their knowledge background, academic teaching skills and scientific research capabilities. This reality may be a good reason to consider ways that the teaching of purpose could be integrated more deliberately into the training of non-ideological and political education teachers. Additionally, there is a need for more research into the specific teaching practices that can support students' purposes, especially from the view of the students themselves.

Limitations of this study should be considered in further research. Purpose measures were initially developed outside of the Chinese context and then adapted to it. This is a common practice and best efforts were made to align purpose definitions, and meaningful Chinese translations and interpretations to the measures; however, measures developed initially within the country might better represent Chinese emic views of purpose. Measurement invariance studies of the purpose, life goals and other measures that have not been widely used would also be informative.

Clearly, many important questions about how young people experience purpose in China and elsewhere are raised from the findings such as: What can account for the fact that upper classman rate their teachers as more purpose supportive? Is it because purpose naturally develops and is more prominent in older people, or rather is it something to do with the efficacy of the college experience itself in which students are immersed over time? If it is the latter, what aspect of that experience is impactful for purpose? This is a question that is pertinent to educators everywhere, and there are many others. Indeed, whether purpose is explicitly or indirectly taught in the curriculum, and whether it is advocated culturally or not in any country, may be a moot point. Overall, this paper would suggest that the study of how teachers and colleges can support young people's positive purposes in life is absolutely critical for young people's development, everywhere.

Acknowledgement

The opinions expressed in this publication are those of the authors and do not necessarily reflect the views of the John Templeton Foundation.

Disclosure statement

No potential conflict of interest was reported by the authors.

Funding

This work was supported in part by a grant to Clark University USA, from the John Templeton Foundation [grant number 43284].

References

Andrews, M. A., K. Rathman, and S. Moran. 2008. "Fostering Purpose in Schools." Unpublished manuscript, Stanford University.

Baumeister, R. F. 1991. *Meanings of Life*. New York: Guilford Press.

Bronk, K. C. 2012. "A Grounded Theory of the Development of Noble Youth Purpose." *Journal of Adolescent Research* 27: 78–109.

Bronk, K. C., and W. H. Finch. 2010. "Adolescent Characteristics by Type of Long-term Aim in Life." *Applied Developmental Science* 14: 35–44.

Bundick, M. J., M. Andrews, A. Jones, J. M., Mariano, K. C. Bronk, and W. Damon. 2006. *Revised Youth Purpose Survey*. Unpublished instrument, Stanford University.

Bundick, M. J., and K. Tirri. 2014. "Student Perceptions of Teacher Support and Competencies for Fostering Youth Purpose and Positive Youth Development: Perspectives from Two Countries." *Applied Developmental Science* 18 (3): 148–162.

Bundick, M. J., D. S. Yeager, P. E. King, and W. Damon. 2010. "Thriving across the Life Span." In *Handbook of Life-span Development*, edited by Richard M. Lerner, M. E. Lamb, A. M. Freund, and W. F. Overton, 882–923. Hoboken, NJ: John Wiley.

Chan, W. C. H. 2014. "Factor Structure of the Chinese Version of the Meaning in Life Questionnaire among Hong Kong Chinese Caregivers." *Health & Social Work* 39 (3): 135–143.

Chen, M. F. 2015. "如何引导大学生树立正确的理想信念." [How to Guide College Students to Build Right Purpose and Belief.] *Frontline* 58 (6): 24-26.

Chen, B., and X. C. Xu. 2011. "教师支持行为及其对初中生自尊水平的影响研究." [Research on Teachers' Supportive Activities and Their Impact on Middle School Students' Self-Esteem Level.] *Journal of Southwest Agricultural University (Social Science Edition)* 9 (6): 199-202. doi: 10.3969/j.issn.1672-5379.2011.06.059.

Cohen, J. 1992. "A Power Primer." *Psychological Bulletin* 112: 155–159.

Cotton Bronk, K. C., P. L. Hill, D. K. Lapsley, T. L. Talib, and H. Finch. 2009. "Purpose, Hope, and Life Satisfaction in Three Age Groups." *The Journal of Positive Psychology* 4 (6): 500–510.

Damon, W. 2008a. "The Moral North Star." *Educational Leadership* 66 (2): 8–13.

Damon, W. 2008b. *The Path to Purpose: How Young People Find Their Calling in Life*. New York: Simon and Schuster.

Damon, W. 2009. *Final Report to the John Templeton Foundation*. Unpublished report, Stanford University.

Damon, W., J. Menon, and K. C. Bronk. 2003. "The Development of Purpose during Adolescence." *Applied Developmental Science* 7 (3): 119–128.

Devogler, K. L., and P. Ebersole. 1980. "Categorization of College Students' Meaning of Life." *Psychological Reports* 46 (2): 387–390.

Devogler, K. L., and P. Ebersole. 1981. "Adults' Meaning in Life." *Psychological Reports* 49: 87–90.

Devogler, K. L., and P. Ebersole. 1983. "Young Adolescents' Meaning in Life." *Psychological Reports* 52 (2): 427–431.

Doerries, L. E. 1970. "Purpose in Life and Social Participation." *Journal of Individual Psychology* 26: 50–53.

Dong, H. 1984. "Arguments on Contemporary Youth's Evaluation on Communist Purpose." *Youth Research* 2: 1–6.

Du, Y. F. 2015. "中学生感知到的教师支持对学业求助的影响." [Effects of Middle School Students' Perceived Teacher Support on Academic Support Seeking.] *Modern Communication* 29: 115–116. doi: 10.3969/j.issn.1009-5349.2015.01.088.

French, S., and S. Joseph. 1999. "Religiosity and Its Association with Happiness, Purpose in Life, and Self-actualisation." *Mental Health, Religion & Culture* 2 (2): 117–120.

Fu, R. C., and C. Q. Guo. 2012. "发挥教师支持作用, 提升学生自学素质." [Teacher's Support and Student's Autonomous Learning Quality.] *Jiangsu Education Research* 29 (1): 57–61.

Gallup and Purdue University. 2014. *Great Jobs, Great Lives: The 2014 Gallup-Purdue Index Report*. Washington, DC: Gallup.

Giddens, A. 1991. *Modernity and Self-identity: Self and Society in the Late Modern Age*. Stanford, CA: Stanford University Press.

Grotevant, H. D. 1987. "Toward a Process Model of Identity Formation." *Journal of Adolescent Research* 2 (3): 203–222.

Guo, T. 2011. "关于新时期加强大学生理想信念教育的思考." [Thoughts on Reinforcing Ideological and Political Education among College Students in the New Era.] *Shaanxi Education (Higher Education)* 4 (12): 120–121.

Hill, P. L., A. L. Burrow, J. W. Brandenberger, D. K. Lapsley, and J. C. Quaranto. 2010. "Collegiate Purpose Orientations and Well-being in Early and Middle Adulthood." *Journal of Applied Developmental Psychology* 31 (2): 173–179.

Jiang, F. 2013. "当代大学生人生理想:样态及影响因素." [Life Purpose of Contemporary Chinese College Students: Developmental Status and Impact Factors.] *Ideological and Theoretical Education* 29 (11): 88–91.

Jiang, H., and R. S. Huang. 2009. "以社会主义核心价值体系引领大学生理想信念教育深入发展." [Guiding the Deep Development of College Students' Purpose and Belief Education with Socialist Core Value System.] *Leading Journal of Ideological & Theoretical Education* 16 (11): 91–94.

Jiang, F., and S. Lin. 2014. "中美大学生人生理想道德属性比较研究." [A Comparative Study on the Moral Orientation of Life Purpose between Chinese and American College Students.] *Journal of Northeastern University (Social Science)* 16 (6): 628–633.

Keyes, C. L., Dov Shmotkin, and C. D. Ryff. 2002. "Optimizing Well-Being: The Empirical Encounter of Two Traditions." *Journal of Personality and Social Psychology* 82 (6): 1007–1022.

King, L. A., J. A. Hicks, J. L. Krull, and A. K. Del Gaiso. 2006. "Positive Affect and the Experience of Meaning in Life." *Journal of Personality and Social Psychology* 90: 179–196.

Kirkcaldy, B., A. Furnham, and G. Siefen. 2004. "The Relationship between Health Efficacy, Educational Attainment, and Well-being among 30 Nations." *European Psychologist* 9 (2): 107–119.

Lerner, R. M. 1982. "Children and Adolescents as Producers of Their Own Development." *Developmental Review* 2 (4):3 42–70.

Li, J., and F. Cui. 2008. "教师职责基本内涵与现代教育理念." [The Basic Connotation of Teachers' Role and Modern Educational Ideas.] *China Higher Education Research* 24: 36–39.

Liu, J. J. 2005. "关于理想信念教育的几点理论思考." [Several Theoretical Thoughts on Purpose and Belief Education.] *Teaching and Research* 11 (11): 14–15. doi: 10.3969/j.issn.0257-2826.2004.11.005.

Malin, H. 2015. "Arts Participation as a Context for Youth Purpose." *Studies in Art Education* 56 (3): 268–280.

Mariano, J. M. 2014. "Introduction to Special Section: Understanding Paths to Youth Purpose – Why Content and Contexts Matter." *Applied Developmental Science* 18 (3): 139–147.

Mariano, J. M., J. Going, K. Schrock, and K. Sweeting. 2011. "Youth Purpose and the Perception of Social Supports among African-American Girls." *Journal of Youth Studies* 14 (8): 921–937.

Markus, H. R., and S. Kitayama. 2010. "Cultures and Selves: A Cycle of Mutual Constitution." *Perspectives on Psychological Science* 5 (4): 420–430.

Massey, E. K., W. A. Gebhardt, and N. Garnefski. 2008. "Adolescent Goal Content and Pursuit: A Review of the Literature from the past 16 Years." *Developmental Review* 28 (4): 421–460.

Moran, C. D. 2001. "Purpose in Life, Student Development, and Well-being: Recommendations for Student Affairs Practitioners." *Journal of Student Affairs Research and Practice* 38 (3): 361–371.

Moran, S. 2014. "What 'Purpose' Means to Youth: Are There Cultures of Purpose?" *Applied Developmental Science* 18 (3): 163–175.

Moran, S., M. J. Bundick, H. Malin, and T. S. Reilly. 2013. "How Supportive of Their Specific Purposes Do Youth Believe Their Family and Friends Are?" *Journal of Adolescent Research* 28 (3): 348–377.

Nicpon, M. F., L. Huser, E. H. Blanks, S. Sollenberger, C. Befort, and S. E. Robinson Kurpius. 2006. "The Relationship of Loneliness and Social Support with College Freshmen's Academic Performance and Persistence." *Journal of College Student Retention: Research, Theory & Practice* 8 (3): 345–358.

Nunnally, J. C. 1978. *Psychometric Theory*. 2nd ed. New York: McGraw-Hill.

Pearson, P. R., and B. F. Sheffield. 1974. "Purpose-in-life and the Eysenck Personality Inventory." *Journal of Clinical Psychology* 30 (4): 562–564.

Reker, G. T., E. J. Peacock, and P. T. Wong. 1987. "Meaning and Purpose in Life and Well-being: A Life-span Perspective." *Journal of Gerontology* 42: 44–49.

Ryff, C. D., and B. Singer. 1998. "Middle Age and Well-Being." In *Encyclopedia of Mental Health*, edited by L. Henderson and P. Zimbardo, 707–719. San Diego, CA: Academic Press.

Seligman, M. E. P. 2002. *Authentic Happiness: Using the New Positive Psychology to Realize Your Potential for Lasting Fulfillment*. New York: Free Press.

Standing Committee of the 9th National People's Congress of the People's Republic of China. 1998. *The Higher Education Law of the People's Republic of China*. Chapter V, Article 47. Beijing: China Law Press.

Steger, M. F. 2012. "Experiencing Meaning in Life." In *The Human Quest for Meaning: Theories, Research, and Applications*. 2nd ed., edited by P. T. P. Wong, 165–184. New York: Routledge.

Steger, M. F., P. Frazier, S. Oishi, and M. Kaler. 2006. "The Meaning in Life Questionnaire: Assessing the Presence of and Search for Meaning in Life." *Journal of Counseling Psychology* 53: 80–93.

Steger, M. F., T. B. Kashdan, B. A. Sullivan, and D. Lorentz. 2008. "Understanding the Search for Meaning in Life: Personality, Cognitive Style, and the Dynamic between Seeking and Experiencing Meaning." *Journal of Personality* 76 (2): 199–228.

Su, L. Y., and X. Z. Feng. 2009. "课堂情境, 教师支持与任务难度对学生学业求助影响的研究." [Research on the Effects of Classroom Context, Teacher Support and Task Difficulty on Students' Academic Help Seeking.] In *Collection of Abstracts of the 12th National Conference on Psychology*, edited by W. X. Zhang, 18. Linfen: Shanxi Normal University.

Tam, C. L., and S. G. Lim. 2009. "Perceived Social Support, Coping Capability and Gender Differences among Young Adults." *Sunway Academic Journal* 6: 75–88.

Thauberger, P. C., and J. F. Cleland. 1981. "Purpose in Life and Some Correlates of Social Behavior and Health." *Journal of Alcohol and Drug Education* 27 (1): 19–25.

Ulmer, Ann, Lillian M. Range, and Peggy C. Smith. 1991. "Purpose in Life: A Moderator of Recovery from Bereavement." *OMEGA-Journal of Death and Dying* 23 (4): 279–289.

Wang, Y. 2011. "增强"90 后"大学生理想信念教育实效性的思考." [On Issues of Raising the Effectiveness of Ideal Belief Education for Post-90 College Students.] *Teaching and Research* 59 (4): 19–22.

Wang, Y., and Y. W. Song. 2011. "新形势下大学生理想信念教育的问题与对策." [Risks and Preventions of College Students' Ideal and Belief Education in the New Circumstance.] *Leadin Journal of Ideological & Theoretical Education* 18 (4): 57–60.

Wang, S. M., and Y. T. Zheng. 2008. "当代大学生理想信念形成特点及原因分析." [Formation of Ideals and Beliefs of Modern University Students: Characteristics and Attributional Analysis.] *Teaching and Research* 56 (5): 74–79. doi: 10.3969/j.issn.0257-2826.2008.05.011.

Wei, H. X. 2015. "大学生理想信念教育培养的协同机制构建 – 整体性视域下." [The Construction of Synergy Mechanism of Purpose and Belief Education among College Students – Under Holistic Perspective.] *Theory Research* 57 (32): 173–175.

White, K. J., L. M. Wagener, and J. L. Furrow. 2009. "Purpose in Adolescence, What Am I Here for?: A Qualitative Examination on the Expression, Development and Integration of Purpose in at-Risk and Thriving Male Adolescents." *International Journal of Existential Psychology and Psychotherapy* 3: 1–16.

Wu, Q. T. 2011. "正确理解理想信念的科学含义." [Properly Understanding the Scientific Meaning of Ideal Beliefs.] *Teaching and Research* 59 (4): 5–9. doi: 10.3969/j.issn.0257-2826.2011.04.001.

Xue, X. L., Z. P. Lin, and J. S. Zheng. 2010. "教师支持在大学生成长中的角色作用." [Impact of Teacher Support on College Student Growth.] *China Journal of Health Psychology* 18 (4): 490–493. doi:10.13342/j.cnki.cjhp.2010.04.051.

Yang, W. P., X. X. Huang, and X. C. Zhu. 2010. "初探当代大学生理想信念和人生追求." [An Exploration of Contemporary College Students' Life Purpose.] *China Electronic Power Education* 26 (6): 159–161. doi:10.3969/j.issn.1007-0079.2010.06.073.

Yarnell, T. D. 1971. "Purpose-in-life Test: Further Correlates." *Journal of Individual Psychology* 27 (1): 76–79.

Yeager, D. S., M. D. Henderson, D. Paunesku, G. M. Walton, S. S. D'Mello, B. J. Spitzer, and A. L. Duckworth. 2014. "Boring but Important: A Self-transcendent Purpose for Learning Fosters Academic Self-regulation." *Journal of Personality and Social Psychology* 107 (4): 559–580.

Zhang, Y. 2006. 现代思想政治教育学 [Modern Ideological and Political Education]. Beijing: People's Publishing House.

Zhang, H. B. 2012. "大学生感知到的教师支持、自我决定动机与学业情绪的关系." [Study on the Relationship of Perception of Teacher's Supporting, Self-determination and Academic Emotions of College Students.] M.A. thesis, Harbin Engineering University.

What do teachers think about youth purpose?

Seana Moran

ABSTRACT

Life purpose combines personal meaning, future intention, active engagement and expected beyond-the-self impact into a self-regulating beacon for decisions and actions. Interest has grown in how teachers could foster youth purpose. Although studies show relationships between pedagogy and purpose, how teachers themselves understand the concept and view their role in its development need more research. This descriptive, qualitative, secondary analysis of observations and comments of teachers in the United States of America during their normal school days can help teacher educators to instil a purpose orientation in pedagogical training. Teachers are interested in purpose for pupils and for themselves. But they are ambivalent about their efficacy to support purpose development. Currently, purpose is often equated with career rather than with a broader life aim. Personal meaning and engagement are easier purpose dimensions for teachers to design activities for pupils to practice, whereas intention and beyond-the-self impact are less often taught or only addressed abstractly. Specific purpose-related activities are shared to provide ideas for other teachers' own purpose pedagogies.

Introduction

Schools worldwide increasingly are being asked to educate for life success and prosocial engagement (Tirri 2012). Pupils are expected not only to learn *that* something is important, but also to learn *why*, including why they as individuals are important to society (Damon 2009). One approach calls for schools to foster the development of life purpose, a stable, long-term aim with four integrated dimensions: personal meaning or emotional significance, intention toward future behaviour, engagement or current actions toward the aim and recognition of the beyond-the-self impact of one's actions and plans (Damon, Menon, and Cotton Bronk 2003). Purpose is a form of self-regulation, which not only can improve individuals' academic achievement (Yeager and Bundick 2009) but also create a future-oriented life pathway for themselves (Nurmi 1991) towards positive well-being (Burrow and Hill 2011).

Since life purpose is an internalised beacon that helps individuals steer their own futures (Moran 2009), the person's subjective framing of their purpose is important (Moran 2014b) and can motivate further learning (Yeager and Walton 2011). A few qualitative studies show

how *youth* think about life purpose (Bronk 2012; Moran 2014b). Less research has addressed *teachers'* subjective understandings of life purpose, although a few studies have used more objective approaches (Bundick and Tirri 2014). Better understanding how teachers view new educational initiatives can have a big impact on those initiatives' success (De Vries and Beijaard 1999; Van den Berg 2002).

This paper describes a secondary analysis of exploratory data collected during observational visits in a small sample of public schools in the United States. The experiences, lessons and activities that teachers considered important for developing youth purpose were coded in relation to Damon's (2008) dimensions of purpose for insights on how teacher educators might make pedagogies for purpose development more central in youth education.

The importance of purpose development to educational effectiveness

Although educating pupils for purpose tends to be viewed as supplementary to academic achievement, it may be the case that purpose development is fundamental for educational effectiveness over the long term. A reciprocal, dynamic relationship between purpose and learning suggests a possible model of educating *for* purpose: schools support pupils to find an individual life purpose, which becomes a mechanism of self-regulation (Moran 2014a). Recent meta-analyses covering two decades of educational effectiveness studies emphasise how important self-regulation is to positive pupil outcomes (Seidel and Shavelson 2007).

Supporting the development of a pupil to self-regulate is not the same as supporting the pupil (Moran et al. 2012). Indeed, these two kinds of support may be antagonistic if supporting the person means making a task easier rather than encouraging mastery (Thoonen et al. 2011). Larson (2006) uses the term 'intentionality paradox' to refer to the challenge for teachers to scaffold pupils' own psychological control rather than to control pupils' behaviour directly. If done skilfully, purpose development transforms pupils from learning consumers into autonomous learning partners (Thoonen et al. 2011). Pupils focus on their purpose to keep themselves on track because they have a vested personal interest in the schoolwork, even if the immediate educational task is not intrinsically interesting to them (Yeager et al. 2014). If teachers can help pupils create a purpose as an internal beacon to give themselves momentum, then the developmental trajectory of a pupil's purpose may serve as an indicator of whether pupils are on the right path.

The importance of education in the development of purpose

Most youths' purposes are normative (Moran 2010), and school is a key institution for promoting normative goals and behaviours (Flum and Kaplan 2006). Schools help pupils explore various pathways to realise valued purposes (Malin et al. 2013), and schools provide mentors, models and opportunities to step onto a particular pathway (Moran et al. 2012).

But the relationship between today's schooling practices and purpose development remains unclear. On one hand, most youth currently do not see a connection between their schooling and their long-term aims (Kiang 2011; Moran et al. 2012). On the other hand, several school-based programmes show life purpose *can* be addressed, e.g. through character education, civic engagement and 'whole child' curricula (Tirri and Ubani 2013).

A key disjunction between educational practices and purpose development is that schools tend not to recognise that purpose has content, *what* the particular person aims to become

(Damon 2008). The content may be: become an astronaut, overcome racism, raise conscientious children and so forth. This content guides the youth's behaviour and maintains momentum despite setbacks (Moran 2014a). The specificity of the purpose can link classroom activities to vested interests in their own futures (Damon 2008).

Yet, schooling in many countries primarily focuses on academics based on *objective* standards and testing that take little heed of pupils' individualised life aims (e.g. Dar 2015; Thoonen et al. 2011). A 'one size fits all' curriculum may not align with the particular purpose contents of pupils (Malin et al. 2013; Moran et al. 2012), which can contribute to pupils discounting the value of lessons to their futures, resulting in missed learning opportunities. Even much of the research on youth purpose uses decontextualised measures that do not consider purpose content (e.g. Steger et al. 2006). If purpose content is recognised, in many countries, that content focuses on career, which limits purpose's relevance to what a young person will do for a living, not who the young person aims to become and why (e.g. Rathman 2005; Schoon 2001; Shin et al. 2014).

Thus, it is not surprising that a few studies suggest that teachers are better at helping youth *without* a purpose to find an interest that might develop into a meaningful intention than at helping youth *with* purpose gather momentum (Bundick 2011). Other studies suggest that some educational practices may help youth with *nascent* purposes find opportunities to engage their aims (Malin et al. 2013; Moran et al. 2012) by seeing the influence of their actions on others (Moran 2010), or deepening their commitment to and integration of the purpose into their various life roles (Bronk 2012). Qualitative analyses and case studies show that the most strongly purposeful youth who do mention schooling as an influence often reflect on how a *teacher*, in particular, was fundamental to the development of their purpose (Bronk 2012; Moran et al. 2012).

The central role of teachers

Researchers argue that teachers *should* take a leadership role in purpose development (Dik et al. 2011; Schachter and Rich 2011). Research on teachers' roles in pupils' self-directedness, autonomy and purposefulness has grown in recent years (Bundick and Tirri 2014; Flores and Niklasson 2014; Reinders and Balcikanli 2011; Schachter and Rich 2011). Overall, the few studies relating pedagogy and teacher characteristics with youth purpose find positive correlations (Mariano 2011).

Teachers provide an interpersonal, emotional dimension to learning (Lam et al. 2014) that can stimulate both personal meaning and beyond-the-self orientation in pupils. Teachers facilitate pupil internal control and self-regulation (Thoonen et al. 2011). Teacher competence for future planning, goal setting, consideration of consequences and emphasis on the importance of schooling can affect how much pupils believe they have a life purpose (Bundick and Tirri 2014).

Furthermore, teachers themselves tend to be purposeful. Statistical studies suggest that people with purposeful motivations are drawn to teaching (Flores and Niklasson 2014). The long-term perspective associated with purpose seems to influence teachers' resilience and motivation to pursue lifelong self-development (Tirri and Ubani 2013). Teachers can serve as role models to inspire pupils and to demonstrate desired behaviour (Dar 2015; Morgenroth, Ryan, and Peters 2015).

Overview of studies

This research is based on data collected as part of a grant-funded, nationwide, four-year study to examine the prevalence, correlates, supports and development of life purpose in young people age 12–22 in the United States of America. The two exploratory, secondary analyses described below convey teachers' pedagogical considerations in relation to the four dimensions of youth purpose (Damon 2008). Study 1 categorises researchers' observations of how teachers perceive opportunities and design practices to address purpose during the school day. Study 2 categories teachers' responses to explicit questions about teaching for purpose development collected during a special in-service training day.

This study is exempt from human subjects research review and consent forms in the United States because it is a secondary analysis on data collected in established educational settings involving normal educational practices, and because information from artefacts on display, conversations and observation of public behaviour did not include personally identifying information. The umbrella study was under a human subjects protocol of the university where the observers were employed.

Study 1: teacher practices: research questions

    (1)   How do teachers understand the dimensions of purpose?
    (2)   In what ways and contexts do teachers address purpose dimensions in their lessons or interactions with pupils?

Method

Sample and data collection

This secondary analysis aims to catalogue teachers' ideas and actions according to Damon's (2008) four dimensions of purpose and to look for patterns in teachers' perspectives and practices to develop youth purpose in schools. Source documents (Andrews, Rathman, and Moran 2008; Rathman 2008) described observations of teacher actions and comments collected by three observers: a male in his 20s, a female in her 30s and a female in her 50s. Collection occurred during visits over two years to a public K-12 rural school in the Rocky Mountains and several New England public schools: one urban and three suburban middle schools, and one suburban and one urban high school.

The original purpose of the visits was to record where, when and how potentially purpose-related ideas or activities were occurring in schools in any grade level or subject matter. School access and participation were coordinated through a non-profit organisation that was working with these schools to enhance 'student aspirations'. School administrators volunteered to have observers sit in on lessons, assemblies, faculty meetings, in-service training, parent–teacher association meetings and special events. Teachers volunteered to host observers in classrooms or activities and to have conversations about their teaching practices and opportunities. Approximately 85 teachers directly interacted with observers over all visits, but more teachers were observed indirectly in large-group events. Teacher comments were not recorded verbatim, and comments were not linked to teacher identities.

EDUCATION FOR PURPOSEFUL TEACHING AROUND THE WORLD

Observers did not have a pre-set interview guide. They were trained to be perceptive, casual and conversational. During classes, they focused on pupil engagement levels and topics of discussions. After classes, observers asked teachers to see lesson plans and pupil work, reflect on pupil responses or projects and share what the teacher considered most important about what happened in the classroom. When observing teacher trainings and meetings, observers noted when and how teachers addressed pupil meaning-making, future prospects, community participation and self-directedness.

Qualitative data analyses

Based on prior work that associates purposefulness with agency (e.g. Bandura et al. 2001; Damon 2008), observations were categorised according to who held the majority of agency in the activity or event:

- decision-makers outside the school, such as policy-makers or district leaders (such as with standardised tests or other externally imposed requirements);
- the school community as a whole (such as with rallies, assemblies or school-community partnerships);
- teachers (such as with lectures and activities for which the teacher makes decisions); and
- pupils (such as individual projects, extracurricular leadership roles and assignments for which pupils can choose the topic).

Because this paper's research questions focus on teachers' roles in purpose development and because youth purpose theory emphasises youths' internal beacons (Damon 2008), only observations of situations in which teacher or pupil was the primary agent were analysed further.

These remaining teacher-agentic or pupil-agentic observations were categorised based on which of the four dimensions of Damon's (2008) purpose definition the observed event aimed to affect. The first 20% of the remaining observations in the collated document were content analysed (Boyatzis 1998; Miles and Huberman 1994) by two coders, achieving 82% reliability. Thereafter, the other 80% of observations were coded by one coder. An observation could be coded as present for none, any or all of the dimensions:

- *Personal meaning* was coded when the observation emphasised pupils' idiosyncratic understandings, values, emotional significance or what pupils' care about. For example, activities in which pupils shared their own perspectives on course content or considered the implications of the material in their own lives were coded as personal meaning. Activities calling for recitation of objective facts, reproducing denotative meanings of words or demonstrating understanding of a pre-defined 'correct' answer were not coded as personal meaning.
- *Intention* was coded when the observation showed pupils focused on their own futures. Activities that involved pupils contemplating 'what could be' scenarios, planning their own work, stating and pursuing goals, articulating why they were pursuing a particular end and connecting current behaviours to later opportunities were coded as intention. Following directions, accidental or random responses, memorisation of facts or activities that lacked anticipation were not coded as intention.

- *Engagement* was coded when the observation involved pupils acting interested or curious, making choices or judgements or taking responsibility. Activities that had a 'gap' requiring pupils to make decisions, solve problems, strategise, transform materials, generate new ideas or otherwise have something at stake in the outcome were coded as engagement. Listening to information, rote activities or lesson formats that gave no opportunity for pupils to act or speak were not coded as engagement.
- *Beyond-the-self impact* was coded when the observation included mechanisms through which pupils' actions were experienced by others, impacted others or required a response from others, ideally in a way that pupils could gather feedback on those impacts. Activities that involved collaboration, presentation of ideas to people other than the teacher, cooperation with people outside the classroom and interaction with community members were coded as beyond-the-self impact. Handing in assignments only to the teacher, activities focused on benefits only to the pupil (e.g. grade or award) or activities where other individuals relevant to the topic or situation are not made salient to the pupil (e.g. raising money for an unknown entity) were not coded as beyond-the-self impact.

Results

Four patterns emerged regarding pedagogical tools teachers considered as helping pupils develop life purpose: 'Purpose is what I already do'; 'I role model purposefulness'; 'I scout real-world opportunities'; and 'I coach pupils to step up'. In the first two patterns, the agency stays clearly with the teachers, but in the second two patterns, the agency segues to the pupils.

Teacher as unchanging: 'purpose is what I already do, but by a different name'

Several teachers thought fostering purpose was a new name for tried-and-true educational strategies. This approach supported thinking *about* purpose. The most common observation was direct instruction of purpose, usually in terms of career guidance. Purpose as its own subject matter in a self-contained unit helped pupils understand the *concept* of purpose, including sub-concepts like goal-setting, planning, values and reasoning. These concepts linked to the intention and meaning dimensions of purpose abstractly, but the dimensions of engagement and effects on others were generally ignored.

Teachers taught pupils to diagram events or consequences that made intellectual connections between present and future or between interests and opportunities. They created bulletin boards or ceremonies that represented pupil intellectual accomplishments. But there was no impetus or venue for pupils to put themselves, as idiosyncratic individuals, into the class content, such as linking academic learning to their lives outside school or to their specific future aims. There were no opportunities for pupils to try real or simulated activities through which they might 'get a feel for' a specific purpose.

Purpose as career guidance involved pupils taking vocational interest or aptitude tests, attending career fairs or shadowing a professional for a day to learn about possible work roles. This approach emphasised intention: what do pupils want to be, or what should they be, when they join the workforce? Teachers helped pupils narrow their interests, tie their

EDUCATION FOR PURPOSEFUL TEACHING AROUND THE WORLD

interests to work fields and reinforced how particular academic skills like math or writing are needed for most jobs. Several teachers noted they felt increased pressure to link class work to careers.

Teacher as role model: 'purpose is a "trickle down" process'

Although a few teachers said they had not found their own life purpose yet, several teachers suggested their role was to be exemplars of purpose. This role modelling incorporated personal meaning and intention, but it focused on the *teacher's* meaning and intentions. For example, some teachers showcased their own specific life purposes by telling stories or leading field trips to influential locations to portray the path they took in life. Other teachers infused their life purpose into units or afterschool clubs, such as jewellery-making or computer gaming.

A few teachers designed activities that allowed pupils to engage with the teacher's life purpose. Sometimes, these activities also made pupils aware of the purpose's beyond-the-self impact. The clearest example was when teachers involved pupils in service projects. One health teacher's unit on infection prevention included pupils helping a charity provide nets to protect children in Africa from malaria infection. A science teacher's unit demonstrated how pupils' actions contributed to nested ecological systems. An art department partnered with a community arts organisation so pupils could contribute to public arts projects.

The role model approach allowed pupils to see teachers as multidimensional adults with lives beyond the teacher role. These teachers provided examples of purposeful behaviour for pupils to emulate. A few teachers invited guest speakers, assigned biographical or autobiographical readings or shared newspaper articles on purposeful people in the community who were relevant to their subject matter so pupils were exposed to a wider variety of purpose exemplars. These other exemplars made salient the beyond-the-self impact dimension of purpose because the talks, books or articles showed how their life aims made a difference to others.

Although a role-modelling approach to purpose development is promising, clarification on how teachers' purposes 'trickle down' to become pupil purposes was lacking. For example, some of the lessons were unclear about the specific objective of the role modelling: were teachers modelling possible purpose contents, or behaviours for finding purpose, or strategies to integrate purpose dimensions or general inspiration for being a 'good person'? Furthermore, the role modelling rarely allowed pupils to explore *their own* meanings, intentions or possible beyond-the-self impacts. Thus, in regards to the *pupils'* purpose development, these activities remained passive.

Teacher as architect of opportunities: 'purpose is finding a place in the world'

High school teachers were more likely than middle school teachers to think purpose involved finding a place to contribute to real-world institutions and communities. Teachers found or designed opportunities for pupils to practice contributing. Thus, this pattern of pedagogy focused clearly on the engagement and beyond-the-self impact dimensions of purpose. The clearest manifestation of this teaching pattern was through internships and service-learning.

One high school's vocational-technical faculty set up actual businesses that employed pupils. A day-care employed pupils to take care of faculty members' children during the work day. A pupil-run café served lunches to faculty and the public. Pupil mechanics fixed faculty members' cars. The wood shop built backyard storage sheds for community residents. Computer repair pupils ran a school-wide help desk. Graphic design pupils created letterhead, business cards and posters for school clubs and community clients. Drafting pupils drew plans that electrician pupils used to install electronics in school rooms built by carpentry pupils and decorated by interior design pupils.

Several schools, including middle schools, promoted community service or rallied behind social causes. The whole school community collected winter coats for needy children, or supported a charity that helps children who had lost their hands or joined an anti-bullying campaign. Teachers recognised how such projects not only developed skills but also helped develop personal meaning (How do my actions affect who I am?) and beyond-the-self impact (How do my actions affect others' well-being?).

However, teachers still stayed in control of the activity design and usually did not tailor experiences or tasks to pupils' budding individual life purposes. Teachers' descriptions of the businesses or community service projects used words like 'pupils can *find* their purposes' rather than tailoring opportunities to pupils who already had an idea of their paths forward. These opportunities were aimed to help purpose *searchers* but not as much to help youth already purposeful. The implicit assumption was that school might help launch a purpose, but it is less facile at supporting an existing purpose.

These real-world opportunities had the potential to address all four dimensions of purpose. However, not all did. For example, fundraising-only projects did not allow pupils to meet the people that benefited from their efforts, thus thwarting the important feedback loop of *experiencing* one's own beyond-the-self impact. The most talked-about projects included this feedback mechanism, such as when pupils received thank you notes from some children who got coats. Furthermore, service projects were more often found in non-academic subject areas, like health class or an advisory period. The impact of, for example, math and language on the service's outcome was less apparent. Finally, these projects tended to be of limited duration rather than continuing, so pupils did not have the opportunity to see growing impact over time. Often due to time constraints, pupils were rarely given time to reflect on these opportunities in relation to their own purposes. So it is unclear whether these experiences clarified into personal meaning or a specific intention to drive further behaviour.

There were not many pedagogical tools at this large scale. Despite the potential of these entrepreneurial or community service opportunities, they involved considerable planning and coordination among several teachers or community members. Most teachers tended to share smaller activities that usually highlighted only one purpose dimension and that could be implemented within a classroom with limited resources. Even at smaller scales, a few teachers were quite clever and creative in their approaches. Below are brief activity prompts for pupils that teachers shared, categorised by purpose dimension (because all of the activities involve pupil action, engagement is not included as a separate category):

(1) To convey pupils' personal meaning with clarity and succinctness:
- Create statements of values and purpose that could be read aloud to the class or recorded and shared more widely.
- Write poems that express or exemplify your purpose in life in different scenarios.

EDUCATION FOR PURPOSEFUL TEACHING AROUND THE WORLD

- Build a character and write a purposeful story for the character, then compare your story with other pupils' stories regarding the effect of the purposes on the story plots.

(2) To extend pupils' intentions further into the future:

- Create a map of life events in your past and how they linked together to show how you became who you are today. Then imagine future events 5, 10, 20, 40 years from now that could reasonably result from these past events: What could happen in your future?
- Design a collage or poster of your past, present and future and how these time periods connect with each other.
- Write a letter of intent for the 'job of life' that explains why you are suited for the job.
- Picture an ideal future for yourself, then plan *backwards* how that ideal future connects to now.
- Set a goal for this week. Keep detailed time sheets of how you use time. At the end of the week, review your time sheets and answer these questions: How effectively did you use your time to achieve the goal? If you relived this past week again, what would you do differently? What did you learn from this exercise about connecting current actions to future opportunities?

(3) To focus pupils on how they influence lives beyond their own:

- Find an elderly person, working professional or other inspirational person and correspond with them about their purpose and how it contributes to others' well-being.
- Research charities or social causes, then select one you consider personally important and write about how and why you could contribute to it.

This list shows that teachers are thinking innovatively about how to infuse the dimensions of purpose into activities that engage pupils. No teacher conveyed a multidimensional portrayal of purpose akin to Damon's (2008) four-dimensional definition. But many teachers conveyed ideas related to at least one of Damon's dimensions.

Teacher as coach: 'purpose is reaching, stretching'

The final pattern is the only one in which the pupils are the most agentic in the activity. They clearly are the 'prime movers' in the situation. Three pedagogical tools were most often mentioned in this pattern: individualised learning programmes in which the pupil was both teacher and learner of a unit not offered within the school's current curriculum; pupil-led events like entrepreneurial career fairs; and peer mentoring in which pupils coached other pupils on solving general life problems.

These teachers understood a need to shift from instructing pupils directly towards coaching pupils so that pupils themselves structure their own pathways. Teachers were still needed to help pupils stay on track and within legal and safety requirements, but they used words like 'support' rather than 'instruct' or 'teach'. Responsibility for these activities lay with *pupils* to cause an effect on themselves or others. Rather than working from an a priori rubric to *evaluate* pupil performance, teachers stayed perceptive to pupils' progress so they could adjust plans, actions or feedback to make the experience *valuable* to the pupil.

The path of each pupil-designed activity differed in regards to which dimension of purpose might come to the fore: some pupils started by developing personal meaning and intention, but had trouble finding ways to engage. Others engaged and found paths to continue in the future, but forgot how they were affecting others. Still others focused on the impact they could have on others without reflecting on what the experience meant to their own development. Most of the teachers using these pedagogical tools admitted that they tended to focus on only one of the purpose dimensions: service-learning teachers on engagement, arts teachers on personal meaning, entrepreneurship/business teachers on intention and planning and vocational-technical teachers on beyond-the-self impact.

Interestingly, the teachers who shared these pupil-agentic projects, which theoretically are most likely to stimulate purpose, also expressed a desire for more training in how to teach for youth purposefulness. Teachers expressed enjoyment of witnessing pupils grow in their agency, intentionality, meaningfulness and contributory potential. But they also shared the anxiety they felt to make sure that 'things worked out ok' when they were not as in control of the outcomes as they would be with more traditional pedagogical methods. One teacher wondered how to overcome the urge to 'step in' with answers or 'smooth over the bumps' when such steps may interfere with pupil agency and purpose development. A final thought that one teacher expressed was: 'I feel like I need to completely retrain myself and my pupils to focus on moving forward toward a goal, not on reaching the goal'. This coaching pattern, in particular, suggests that perhaps educating for purpose is to instil in pupils the momentum to reach continually toward something worthy.

Study 2: teacher responses: research questions

(1) How do teachers view their own life purpose and the supports they received to develop it?
(2) What actions do teachers currently take that they believe foster purpose in pupils?
(3) What else do teachers think they could do to help pupils develop life purpose?

Method

Sample and measure

Near the end of the second year of school visits in New England, approximately 200 teachers and administrators attended a district-wide, in-service training session focused on a whole-child approach to education. Observers directly introduced to teachers the concept of life purpose, its four dimensions and recent research findings about it. The observers asked teachers to complete a short worksheet. Anonymously, 131 participants (66%) submitted responses to three prompts:

(1) How did you discover your own purpose in life? Who supported you? What role did school play?
(2) How do you develop/nurture/support purpose in the pupils with whom you work? List at least three concrete ways that educators can help pupils find and pursue their purpose in life.
(3) Given our conversation today, what might you do differently, more deeply or in addition to what you currently do in order to help your pupils discover their purpose?

Qualitative data analyses

Responses to the first question were binary coded by the author (1 if mentioned, 0 if not) for (a) whether school was mentioned as supportive or adverse to their purpose development; (b) whether school played a major or minor role in their own purpose development; (c) whether their own teachers served as a positive or negative influence; (d) whether purpose was discovered while in school or later as an adult; and (e) whether they were still searching for a life purpose.

Responses to the second question were binary coded for particular tactics: (a) caring for the pupil as an individual; (b) encouraging pupils to pursue their ambitions; (c) providing career guidance; (d) providing opportunities for pupils to engage their purposes; (e) tying pupil interests to the 'real world'; (f) providing tools or activities for pupils' independent self-exploration; (g) engaging in conversations directly addressing purpose or the future; (h) helping others; (i) providing ways for pupils to interact with and support each other; (j) role modelling purposefulness; (k) providing activities for pupils to reflect on their actions and plans.

Responses to the third question were binary coded using the same categories as the second question, plus on additional tactic that emerged: (l) focusing on behaviours that do not directly address or involve pupils, such as policy, initiatives, school structure, staff development, advisory programmes or parental involvement.

The coded responses for questions 2 and 3 were further categorised according to the four dimensions of purpose:

- *Personal meaning*: caring for pupils; supporting pupils' self-exploration to understand themselves better.
- *Intention*: encouraging pupils to pursue ambitions; providing career guidance; directly addressing purpose or the future; pupils' reflecting on their actions and plans.
- *Engagement*: providing opportunities to engage purposes; tying pupil interests to the 'real world'.
- *Beyond-the-self impact*: helping others; providing pupil interactions and peer support.

Role modelling purposefulness and focusing on initiatives not directly tied to pupils were not linked to the four dimensions of purpose because they do not focus on pupils.

Results

Teachers' own purpose development

See Table 1. Teachers tended to consider their purpose development as a process of 'experimentation' or 'discovery' or 'trial and error' that involved 'ongoing evolution' through several life experiences 'until I found my niche' or realised 'where I belong'. A little 'guidance' or 'acknowledgement of what I was doing' plus 'luck' that 'opportunities presented themselves' led to a 'realisation'. For a few teachers, there was an early anchor: 'I always loved school'; or 'I have always worked with children'; or 'when K was born and H had issues, it was all about helping children change their lives for the better'; or 'by having a younger brother with speech and language difficulties'. For a few teachers (7%), the search for a purpose still continued: 'Funny question because it assumes I have an answer'. One teacher suggested there was unlikely to be an end: 'The more I see of the world the less I'm all about the answer'.

EDUCATION FOR PURPOSEFUL TEACHING AROUND THE WORLD

Table 1. Influences on teachers' purpose development.

Teachers' purpose development	Respondents who mentioned (%)
School was major positive influence on teacher's purpose	27%
School was minor positive influence	8%
School was not an influence	5%
School was a negative 'anti' influence	2%
Former teacher was positive influence	21%
Former teacher was negative influence	3%
Teacher found purpose as youth (while still in school)	45%
Teacher found purpose as adult (after school)	32%
Teacher is uncertain or searching for purpose	7%

Note: N = 131. Question presented to teachers during a districtwide in-service training session. Responses do not add to 100% because some teachers mentioned non-school supports or had missing or unintelligible responses.

Most teachers considered their teaching job as their purpose. This result is expected, given the general correspondence between purpose and career in most teachers' thinking. However, two other purpose contents were mentioned that made teaching instrumental to a larger purpose. First was having children of one's own, which sometimes was a catalyst for becoming a teacher or made teaching an extension of supporting their families: 'by watching my children as babies'; 'my child being born and the prospect of that future was huge'; 'supporting my family's aspirations'. Second was having a more abstract purpose that gave a 'why' for the act of teaching, such as to impact lives positively, support human rights, or improve children's chances, whereby teaching became the vehicle to achieve the larger purpose: 'support kids to make them feel their voice is important'; 'help others work through issues that are preventing them from realising their full potential'; 'laughter, peace and politics'.

Teaching was most often pursued because the teachers loved children, or enjoyed early opportunities to work with children as babysitters or camp counsellors or tutors, or they were good at school. In other words, engagement drove intention: teachers tried an activity, which they enjoyed or excelled in, and then they created an intention to continue or expand that activity into a career.

One in 10 teachers mentioned how their own children stimulated pursuit of teaching. A few mentioned that they entered teaching after they left another field, which suggests a shift in purpose, such as being 'laid off my blue collar job and had nowhere to go', or finding a new context to enact a more general purpose, such as 'after working in business for a number of years I came to the realisation that education would make a longer lasting positive impact on society'.

As might be expected, almost half (42%) of teachers mentioned school as playing a role in their own life purpose development. College and high school memories were recalled more often as examples. But a few teachers mentioned events in elementary school that were pivotal, such as 'in first grade I retaught the lessons to students who did not understand and have been teaching ever since'. Only 2% named school as a negative influence, noting they became teachers to rectify or counteract adversity they suffered as pupils: 'I hated school, I knew that I could make it more fun'; 'Mrs. B was rude to me in 8th grade'. Some were ambivalent: 'school provided opportunities, opened doors, but has also limited me by keeping things "uniform"'.

About one-third considered school a positive influence, by developing skills, allowing reflection, validating identity and sometimes providing a safe haven. About a quarter (27%)

EDUCATION FOR PURPOSEFUL TEACHING AROUND THE WORLD

Table 2. What teachers said they currently or would consider doing to develop youth purpose.

Teachers' purpose-related practices	Current (%)	Consider (%)
Care about pupil (personal meaning)	65	34
Provide opportunities (engagement)	32	15
Encourage pupil ambitions (intention)	29	7
Promote pupil self-exploration (personal meaning)	21	2
Directly talk about purpose/future (intention)	21	19
Help others (beyond-the-self)	15	3
Role-model purposefulness (n/a)	11	7
Give career guidance (intention)	5	3
Give reality check (engagement)	4	0
Design pupil–pupil interaction (beyond-the-self)	4	2
Promote reflection/why perspective (intention)	4	2
Non-pupil focus, e.g. committees, policy (n/a)		26

Note: $N = 131$. Questions presented to teachers during a districtwide in-service training session. Responses do not add to 100% because, although the question asked for three specific practices, teachers varied in both the quantity and focus of practices. Synonymous practices were counted only once (e.g. 'show I care' and 'build personal relationship' were both categorised as 'care').

thought school was a major influence: 'literature and reading was a raft I clung to in difficult times', or 'people were there who believed in me' or 'making it cool for a girl to be smart and encouraging my ambitions'. Another 8% thought school was a minor influence: 'school gave me the tools … but not in discovering my purpose' or 'only in observation of teachers working with me'. One in five respondents said their own teachers helped them choose the teaching profession, often because their former teachers were models to emulate or explicitly encouraged them. Only 3% mentioned that a former teacher modelled what they wanted *not* to become. Although almost half of respondents realised they wanted to be in education while pupils, another third did not focus on teaching until adulthood.

In summary, many but not all of these teachers saw their profession as a 'calling' and pursued it to help young people, most often by following the teaching patterns they observed and liked when they were pupils. Teaching was a way for them to 'pay forward' their own good experiences in school to the next generation.

Teachers' current and imagined future efforts

See Table 2. Teachers' self-reported current efforts to foster youth purpose clustered into three patterns that emphasised *how* the teacher was interacting with pupils. The strongest pattern was *relational*, which included caring, encouragement, connecting to pupils through role modelling, exemplifying purposefulness and forging positive pupil-to-pupil relations. By far, the top effort (65%) was caring for the pupil as a person. This pattern focuses primarily on *teacher*-as-agent: teachers bestowed something valuable on the pupils, such as to offer an open ear for listening, to 'encourage their talents and dreams', to 'believe in them even when they don't' or to 'have lunch with kids'. The most repeated word in responses was 'listen'.

The second pattern was *behavioural*, which focuses on *pupils*-as-agents, such as by demonstrating specific hands-on opportunities, prosocial acts and self-exploration. Teachers played a supporting role, such as finding opportunities (32%) and encouraging pupil actions (29%). They guided, coached or set up pupils actions: 'finding resources' or seeking chances for pupils to 'practice their interests'. Similar comments included: 'I give the kids in my class

EDUCATION FOR PURPOSEFUL TEACHING AROUND THE WORLD

Table 3. Relational, behavioural and informational patterns for addressing purpose's dimensions.

Purpose dimension	Pattern		
	Relational	Behavioural	Informational
Personal meaning	Care for pupil	Self-explore	
Intention	Encourage ambition		Talk about future
			Career guidance
			Reflect/why
Engagement		Opportunities	Reality check
Beyond-the-self impact	Pupil interactions	Help others	

choice', 'placing pupils in a variety of roles', 'exposure' to contexts, 'allow pupils to mentor younger pupils' or 'everyone has something to offer … find some form of success'.

The least mentioned pattern was *informational*, focusing on traditional teacher tasks: directly teaching or talking about purpose, providing reflection exercises, giving career guidance and serving as a 'reality check' on pupils' aims. These comments were often in shorthand with little elaboration: 'provide information', 'obtain books on certain subjects' or 'define purpose overtly'.

When considering future tactics they might try, many teachers emphasised doing more of what they already do. One in three teachers considered caring more about pupils: 'be more visible' or 'talking about what they enjoy'. Teaching purpose through formal lessons was mentioned by one in five: 'asking the question "what do you want to do when you grow up?"' or 'bulletin boards to initiate discussion about their purpose in life' or 'future planning with pupils'. The only other consideration mentioned by more than 10% was to provide hands-on opportunities (experiential learning): 'give more opportunities for pupils to relate learning to their lives', 'give pupils jobs', 'expand afterschool activities', 'student council, student store., etc., examples of ways to further involve kids to the school' or 'do more community service with kids'. One in four focused future possible actions on what *others* could do, such as task forces, policy-makers or other staff.

As with study 1, teacher efforts also were categorised 'top down' in relation to Damon's (2008) four dimensions of purpose. In current practices, personal meaning was most often supported: teachers caring about pupils as individuals (65%) and promoting pupil self-exploration (21%). Intention also was well supported: teachers encouraging pupils to pursue ambitions (29%) or directly talking about purpose and the future (21%). Engagement was moderately supported: teachers providing opportunities (32%). Beyond-the-self impact was least supported: helping others (15%).

See Table 3. Looking at 'teacher view' and 'researcher view' categorisations simultaneously in a cross-table, it becomes more obvious the difficulty of overcoming traditional educational formats. The only cell with more than one practice is an informational focus on intention by providing a few ways to talk about the future. Yet, the table also shows promise for how teachers are already enacting ways to address the four dimensions of purpose, even if they do not yet use the researchers' specific language about the dimensions.

Discussion

This paper's contributions focus on: (a) teachers' concrete pedagogical examples of purpose-related activities; (b) the categorisation and analysis of teacher experiences and suggestions along the four dimensions of youth purpose; and (c) linking the youth purpose and teacher-focused educational effectiveness scholarship. Although the studies in this paper are of limited generalisability and are not conclusive because of the selective sample and anonymity of data, they can launch further discussion among researchers and practitioners on how to develop better practices to address purpose development. The findings provide a real-world snapshot of teachers' perceived options, thinking and actions to invest proactively in purpose-related endeavours.

Teachers often teach as they were taught, so teacher training has long-term implications for educating future generations (Thoonen et al. 2011). Interest and momentum are growing in teachers' power to make education more purpose oriented. Despite a general sense that purpose is not yet well infused into public schooling, teachers shared many encouraging ideas and practices with the research observers. Several teachers wanted to become more purposeful in their own work and lives. Several teachers wanted to take a longer term perspective and see their teaching efforts blossom for pupils long after pupils leave school. Several teachers already were experimenting with lesson designs to support dimensions of purpose more directly.

This paper suggests concrete ways *how* teachers are important, thus augmenting past survey-based studies (Bundick and Tirri 2014), dilemma-based cases (Seider 2012) and pupil interview studies (Moran et al. 2012) suggesting that teachers are important for purpose development. Most of the findings here corroborate other findings, such as the usefulness of particular purpose-related lessons, for example, on goal-setting and future orientation (Bundick and Tirri 2014); developing emotional maturity, prosocial skills and pupil self-regulation (Dar 2015; Flanagan 2015; Thoonen et al. 2011); and serving as opportunity 'scouts' and foresightful 'guides' into the future (Moran et al. 2012).

The teachers' ideas and perspectives presented here offer several opportunities for teacher educators to create a more coherent curriculum for purpose education. First, teachers pass along what they have experienced from their own schooling and past teachers. Thus, it is important for purpose to be part of teacher training so teachers consider purpose development as part of their job. Second, although teaching may be a generally purposeful vocation (Flores and Niklasson 2014), some teachers still struggle to define their own purpose in life or feel they don't have a language for purpose, so they are hesitant teaching it. Time during teacher training that allows novice teachers to reflect on their own life paths may create a strong emotional as well as intellectual foundation for guiding pupils to do the same. Third, teachers tend to conflate supporting a pupil's purpose (helping them become self-directed and self-regulating) with supporting or caring for a pupil (making them feel they belong and are valued members of a community). They express a desire for more guidance on how to turn over responsibility to the pupils to seek personal meaning, reflect on experiences and forge paths to their future. More training in 'coaching' pedagogy may be helpful, allowing teachers to practice being perceptive and responsive to the process of developing purposes.

Perhaps most far reaching in its implications, teachers expect themselves and their pupils to stay focused on the requirements of the immediate lesson or activity with its objective and prescribed outcome for the pupil. This short-term, self-oriented focus can mute the connection between current learning and long-term, personally meaningful life purpose that contributes to something larger than pupils' immediate needs. First, the future is often considered an abstraction that can be addressed 'later' because it is always at least a day away. One benefit of a life purpose is that it gives the future a concrete picture to help teachers and pupils remember what is coming next. This picture can be a powerful motivator for pupils to persevere despite difficulty or setbacks (Moran 2014a). Second, teachers refer to 'community' as something to build and cherish. But their language sometimes focuses on 'providing' community for pupils rather than pupils 'contributing' community. Community is considered context rather than a product of individuals interacting. Thus, even if pupils are exposed to the idea of purpose, they often are not given opportunities to contribute to something larger than their own learning.

Framing feedback as reflection and evaluation of pupils' actual *contributions* at school highlights how pupils matter to the community. As they learn new skills and behaviours, they can contribute even more. Instead of purpose being exemplified only as career, with a resultant focus on opportunities that are encountered later in life, a contributory pedagogy allows teachers and pupils both to practice and exemplify purpose every day while still in school. The temporal disconnect in teachers' practices between 'learn now' and 'be purposeful later' may cause confusion for pupils. Teacher responses in Study 2, for example, showed that even teachers' descriptions of how their own purposes developed was an interactive, reciprocal, social process between events, experiences, reflection, opportunity, meaning-making and commitment *over time*. Series of 'nows' are the building blocks of what is possible 'later'.

Based on these two studies' findings, and with the intent of helping teacher educators develop 'next steps' in educating for purpose, two specific strategies are suggested: integrating the purpose dimensions to help pupils understand how they are related and build upon each other; and structuring lessons and activities based on pupils' applying learning to make contributions. These strategies do not repeat findings or define best practices, but rather suggest possibilities for teacher educators to build upon the findings in concrete ways.

Help teachers integrate the purpose dimensions

In general, teachers understood the four dimensions of purpose as *independent* concepts. There were ideas to address personal meaningfulness, *or* intentions and future visioning, *or* hands-on engagement *or* prosocial effect. Teachers considered 'meaning' as pupil's self-exploration and communication of opinions; 'intention' as self-efficacy and planning; 'engagement' as completion of assigned tasks, or sometimes real-world opportunities, or occasionally as pupils' taking full responsibility of a project. Teachers considered 'beyond-the-self impact' mostly in terms of their own behaviours, such as caring for pupils and belonging to the school community.

A few educational programmes, such as vocational-technical programmes or similar real-world experiences (Rathman 2008), incorporated *all* the dimensions of purpose: the work was personally meaningful and intentional because pupils *chose* the courses based on interest and expected future career. The work was engaging as pupils solved problems when they arose, and learned to deal with both disappointments and achievements. The work had beyond-the-self impact as pupils felt responsible for outcomes.

Despite this integration of purpose dimensions from an outsider perspective, the teachers themselves hadn't yet realised how these experiences tapped so many dimensions of purpose. Thus, the teachers still tended to focus on the 'parts' rather than the 'whole' of purpose development. Yet, these programmes may be the 'path of least resistance' for introducing purpose within schools since the primary aspect lacking is an introduction of a purpose framework and purpose language (Andrews, Rathman, and Moran 2008). The structure, activities, individualised experiences and pupil agency already exist. Plus, past research suggests that teachers tend to enjoy experiential and problem-based learning formats more than passive traditional formats (Ribeiro 2011).

However, purpose education is likely to spread more widely through schools if it is not limited to special programmes. There seemed a strong need and desire to clarify how fostering purpose can be built up from its dimensional 'building blocks' by integrating simpler activities that teachers already recommended. For example, assignments addressing personal meaning and beyond-the-self orientation could be repeated every quarter. At the end of the year, pupils could analyse changes in their responses over the year, then imagine their further development into the next school year to strengthen their skill in intentionality. Such guided reflective practices are considered powerful for purpose development (Bundick 2011). Indeed, it is important for pupils to have the opportunity to reflect on experiential learning opportunities to understand how they might contribute to pupils' *own* future plans or life purpose (Bundick 2011), which would be important to solidify such short-term engagements into *personally* meaningful pursuits (Moran 2015). Even instilling a habit in teachers and pupils to contemplate 'why' a task should be done can be helpful for finding or strengthening purpose because it puts the purpose in a wider context (Damon 2009).

Integration of purpose dimensions within and/or across activities can help solidify all of the dimensions. Some dimensions, such as personal meaning and engagement, were easier to conceptually grasp and to practice. They are easier to feel via emotions and to see via actions. More difficult are intention and beyond-the-self impact because they require imagining and perceiving the future and others' perspectives. Small changes in lessons may be helpful. For example, rather than teachers trying to convince all pupils that the material is *generally* important, they could encourage pupils to individualise lessons. Teachers provide space for pupils to make lessons 'their own' by tying them to their own *specific* purposes. Similarly, rather than teachers justifying the value of education in terms of pupils' self-centred benefit of 'getting' an education, they could orient pupils toward a positive contribution to the wider world, which simultaneously develops pupils' meaning-making skills and other-focused perspective-taking skills.

Help teachers structure lessons as contributions to others

It may be helpful for teachers to structure lessons around pupil *contributions* (what pupils do that impacts others). Structuring opportunities for pupils to *apply* subject matter and skills in making a contribution addresses all four of purpose's dimensions. This strategy also solidifies learning *why* knowledge and skills are important because pupils can evaluate the results of their contributions. Contribution goes beyond activity (hands-on or social interaction) and engagement (being interested and effortful in tasks) to include producing a beneficial outcome for one's own and others' well-being.

A contribution mindset makes salient the distinctions between who acts (agency), who benefits (impact) and long-term influence (momentum). Contribution reinforces the experience of persons-in-community (Flanagan 2015). Successful purpose development means teachers allow pupils to take responsibility for the effects of their choices and behaviour

(Thoonen et al. 2011). Training may be required to instil dispositions in teachers to allow pupils to perceive opportunities and community needs, act, gather feedback, reflect and make new meaning, solidify or adjust the purpose and repeat the process (Moran 2014a).

Although purpose is a cognitive representation of a person's desired future, it is supported and strengthened through emotional interaction and feedback from others (Malin et al. 2013; Moran 2014a). Purpose makes clearer how a person *matters* to others and a community. Teachers clearly matter to school communities, and many teachers in the sample took on the responsibility of being role models. Teachers repeatedly noted that they are at the 'heart' of education: the personal interaction between teachers and pupils provides emotional tenor to schooling (Lam et al. 2014). Teachers' caring is a stronger predictor than content knowledge or pedagogical skill for pupil school success (Dar 2015) and is strongly related to later community engagement (Flanagan 2015). Plus, teachers with more caring attitudes tend to be more excited about teaching (De Vries and Beijaard 1999) and developing their own teaching purposes (De Vries et al. 2014). Teachers' pedagogical strengths rely on emotional competence, not just cognitive skills, to stimulate empathy or prosociality (Dar 2015). Teachers can role model contribution, but they need to be clear what effects they want to have on pupils (Morgenroth, Ryan, and Peters 2015). At some point, the role-modelling must segue to pupils taking on the roles so that pupils' self-regulation can develop and pupils can perceive and evaluate feedback on their own contributions. This segue shifts the focus from *teachers'* to *pupils'* meanings and intentions. That is when purpose development can take off.

Acknowledgements

Data for this study were collected by the Youth Purpose Project at the Stanford Center on Adolescence under the direction of William Damon, Principal Investigator, funded in part by the John Templeton Foundation and the Thrive Foundation for Youth. The opinions expressed in this publication are those of the author and do not necessarily reflect the views of the John Templeton Foundation.

Disclosure statement

No potential conflict of interest was reported by the author.

Funding

This work was supported by the John Templeton Foundation [grant number 43284].

References

Andrews, M., K. Rathman, and S. Moran. 2008. *Fostering Purpose: A List of Ideas*. Youth Purpose Project, Stanford University. Unpublished working document.

Bandura, A., C. Barbaranelli, G. V. Caprara, and C. Pastorelli. 2001. "Self-Efficacy Beliefs as Shapers of Children's Aspirations and Career Trajectories." *Child Development* 72 (1): 187–206. doi:10.1111/1467-8624.00273.

Boyatzis, R. E. 1998. *Transforming Qualitative Information: Thematic Analysis and Code Development*. Thousand Oaks, CA: Sage.

Bronk, K. C. 2012. "A Grounded Theory of the Development of Noble Youth Purpose." *Journal of Adolescent Research* 27 (1): 78–109.

EDUCATION FOR PURPOSEFUL TEACHING AROUND THE WORLD

Bundick, M. J. 2011. "The Benefits of Reflecting on and Discussing Purpose in Life in Emerging Adulthood." *New Directions for Youth Development* 2011 (132): 89–103.

Bundick, M. J., and K. Tirri. 2014. "Student Perceptions of Teacher Support and Competencies for Fostering Youth Purpose and Positive Youth Development: Perspectives from Two Countries." *Applied Developmental Science* 18 (3): 148–162. doi:10.1080/10888691.2014.924357.

Burrow, A. L., and P. L. Hill. 2011. "Purpose as a Form of Identity Capital for Positive Youth Adjustment." *Developmental Psychology* 47 (4): 1196–1206.

Damon, W. 2008. *The Path to Purpose: Helping Our Children Find Their Calling in Life*. New York: Free Press.

Damon, W. 2009. "The Why Question: Teachers Can Instil a Sense of Purpose." *Education Next* 9 (3): 84.

Damon, W., J. Menon, and K. Cotton Bronk. 2003. "The Development of Purpose during Adolescence." *Applied Developmental Science* 7 (3): 119–128. doi:10.1207/S1532480XADS0703_2.

Dar, F. R. 2015. "Rethinking Education – Emerging Roles for Teachers." *Universal Journal of Educational Research* 3 (2): 63–74.

De Vries, Y., and D. Beijaard. 1999. "Teachers' Conceptions of Education: A Practical Knowledge Perspective on 'Good' Teaching." *Interchange* 30 (4): 371–397.

De Vries, S., E. P. W. A. Jansen, M. Helms-Lorenz, and W. J. C. M. van de Grift. 2014. "Student Teachers' Beliefs about Learning and Teaching and Their Participation in Career-Long Learning Activities." *Journal of Education for Teaching* 40 (4): 344–358. doi:10.1080/02607476.2014.924647.

Dik, B. J., M. F. Steger, A. Gibson, and W. Peisner. 2011. "Make Your Work Matter: Development and Pilot Evaluation of a Purpose-Centered Career Education Intervention." *New Directions for Youth Development* 2011: 59–73.

Flanagan, C. 2015. "Youth Finding Meaning through a Larger Sense of Community." *American Journal of Orthopsychiatry* 85 (6, Suppl): S70–S78.

Flores, M. A., and L. Niklasson. 2014. "Why Do Student Teachers Enrol for a Teaching Degree? A Study of Teacher Recruitment in Portugal and Sweden." *Journal of Education for Teaching* 40 (4): 328–343. doi:10.1080/02607476.2014.929883.

Flum, H., and A. Kaplan. 2006. "Exploratory Orientation as an Educational Goal." *Educational Psychologist* 41 (2): 99–110.

Kiang, L. 2011. "Deriving Daily Purpose through Daily Events and Role Fulfillment among Asian American Youth." *Journal of Research on Adolescence* 22 (1): 185–198.

Lam, S., S. Jimerson, B. P. H. Wong, E. Kikas, H. Shin, F. H. Veiga, C. Hatzichristou, et al. 2014. "Understanding and Measuring Student Engagement in School: The Results of an International Study from 12 Countries." *School Psychology Quarterly* 29 (2): 213–232.

Larson, R. 2006. "Positive Youth Development, Willful Adolescents, and Mentoring." *Journal of Community Psychology* 34 (6): 677–689.

Malin, H., T. S. Reilly, B. Quinn, and S. Moran. 2013. "Adolescent Purpose Development: Exploring Empathy, Discovering Roles, Shifting Priorities, and Creating Pathways." *Journal of Research on Adolescence* 24 (1): 186–199. doi:10.1111/jora.12051.

Mariano, J. M. 2011. "Conclusion: Recommendations for How Practitioners, Researchers, and Policymakers Can Promote Youth Purpose." *New Directions for Youth Development* 2011: 105–111. doi:10.1002/yd.431.

Miles, M. B., and A. M. Huberman. 1994. *Qualitative Data Analysis: An Expanded Sourcebook*. 2nd ed. Thousand Oaks, CA: Sage.

Moran, S. 2009. "Purpose: Giftedness in Intrapersonal Intelligence." *High Ability Studies* 20 (2): 143–159. doi:10.1080/13598130903358501.

Moran, S. 2010. "Changing the World: Tolerance and Creativity Aspirations among American Youth." *High Ability Studies* 21 (2): 117–132.

Moran, S. 2014a. "The Reciprocity of Service and Purpose." Paper presented at the International Conference on Education Research, Seoul, South Korea, October 15–17.

Moran, S. 2014b. "What 'Purpose' Means to Youth: Are There Cultures of Purpose?" *Applied Developmental Science* 18 (3): 163–175. doi:10.1080/10888691.2014.924359.

Moran, S. 2015. "Adolescent Aspirations for Change: Creativity as a Life Purpose." *Asia Pacific Education Review* 16 (2): 167–175. doi:10.1007/s12564-015-9363-z.

EDUCATION FOR PURPOSEFUL TEACHING AROUND THE WORLD

Moran, S., M. J. Bundick, H. Malin, and T. S. Reilly. 2012. "How Supportive of Their Specific Purposes Do Youth Believe Their Family and Friends Are?" *Journal of Adolescent Research* 28 (3): 348–377. doi:10.1177/0743558412457816.

Morgenroth, T., M. K. Ryan, and K. Peters. 2015. "The Motivational Theory of Role Modeling: How Role Models Influence Role Aspirants' Goals." *Review of General Psychology* 19 (4): 465–483.

Nurmi, J.-E. 1991. "How Do Adolescents See Their Future? A Review of the Development of Future Orientation and Planning." *Developmental Review* 11: 1–59.

Rathman, K. 2005. "Education, Self-Knowledge and Life-Planning: Why Schools Should Help Students Decide 'Who' rather than Just 'What' They Want to Be." Master thesis, University of London.

Rathman, K. 2008. *Review of COA Educational Partnership and Ideas for Future COA Project*. Youth Purpose Project, Stanford University. Unpublished document.

Reinders, H., and C. Balcikanli. 2011. "Learning to Foster Autonomy: The Role of Teacher Education Materials." *Studies in Self-Access Learning Journal* 2 (1): 15–25.

Ribeiro, L. R. C. 2011. "The Pros and Cons of Problem-based Learning from the Teacher's Standpoint." *Journal of University Teaching and Learning Practice* 8 (1): 1–17.

Schachter, E. P., and Y. Rich. 2011. "Identity Education: A Conceptual Framework for Educational Researchers and Practitioners." *Educational Psychologist* 46 (4): 222–238.

Schoon, I. 2001. "Teenage Job Aspirations and Career Attainment in Adulthood: A 17-Year Follow-up Study of Teenagers Who Aspired to Become Scientists, Health Professionals, or Engineers." *International Journal of Behavioral Development* 25 (2): 124–132.

Seidel, T., and R. J. Shavelson. 2007. "Teaching Effectiveness Research in the Past Decade: The Role of Theory and Research Design in Disentangling Meta-Analysis Results." *Review of Educational Research* 77 (4): 454–499.

Seider, S. 2012. *Character Compass*. Cambridge, MA: Harvard Educational Press.

Shin, J., H. Hwang, E. Cho, and A. McCarthy-Donovan. 2014. "Current Trends in Korean Adolescents' Social Purpose." *Journal of Youth Development* 9 (2): 16–33.

Steger, M. F., P. Frazier, S. Oishi, and M. Kaler. 2006. "The Meaning in Life Questionnaire: Assessing the Presence of and Search for Meaning in Life." *Journal of Counseling Psychology* 53: 80–93.

Thoonen, E. E. J., P. J. C. Sleegers, F. J. Oort, T. T. D. Peetsma, and F. P. Geijsel. 2011. "How to Improve Teaching Practices: The Role of Teacher Motivation, Organizational Factors, and Leadership Practices." *Educational Administration Quarterly* 47 (3): 496–536.

Tirri, K. 2012. "The Core of School Pedagogy: Finnish Teachers' Views of the Educational Purposefulness of Their Teaching." In *Miracle of Education*, edited by H. Niemi, A. Toom, and A. Kallioniemi, 55–66. Rotterdam: Sense.

Tirri, K., and M. Ubani. 2013. "Education of Finnish Student Teachers for Purposeful Teaching." *The Journal for the Education of Teaching* 39 (1): 21–29.

Van den Berg, R. 2002. "Teachers' Meanings Regarding Educational Practice." *Review of Educational Research* 72 (4): 577–625.

Yeager, D. S., and M. J. Bundick. 2009. "The Role of Purposeful Work Goals in Promoting Meaning in Life and in Schoolwork during Adolescence." *Journal of Adolescent Research* 24 (4): 423–452.

Yeager, D. S., M. Henderson, D. Paunesku, G. Walton, S. D'Mello, B. J. Spitzer, and A. L. Duckworth. 2014. "Boring but Important: A Self-Transcendent Purpose for Learning Fosters Academic Self-Regulation." *Journal of Personality and Social Psychology* 107: 559–580.

Yeager, D. S., and G. Walton. 2011. "Social-Psychological Interventions in Education: They're Not Magic." *Review of Educational Research* 81: 267–301.

Learning from the wisdom of practice: teachers' educational purposes as pathways to supporting adolescent purpose in secondary classrooms

Brandy P. Quinn

ABSTRACT

Purpose in life is beneficial for adolescents and their communities. However, less is known about supports for purpose development during adolescence, particularly in the school setting. The study described here drew from theories about teacher beliefs and knowledge, and a multidimensional definition of purpose in life, in order to learn from practising teachers about the ways in which supporting adolescent purpose may fit within their existing beliefs about their work with students. The specific aims were to explore alignment between teachers' educational purposes and their own definitions of purpose in life with the 'personal meaning' and 'beyond-the-self' dimensions of purpose in life. Nine secondary school teachers from the United States who taught in a variety of academic content areas were interviewed using a semi-structured protocol. Transcripts were coded according to two dimensions of purpose: personal meaning and beyond-the-self consequences. Teacher responses revealed alignment between their educational purposes and the dimensions of 'personal meaning' and 'beyond-the-self consequences'. At the same time, teacher definitions of the unified construct of purpose in life did not reflect this same integration of the dimensions of purpose. Implications for teacher education and future research are discussed.

Introduction

Within adolescent developmental research, purpose in life has been defined as 'a long-term intention to accomplish something that is at once meaningful to the self and of consequence to the world beyond the self' (Damon, Menon, and Bronk 2003, 21). While researchers in the field of positive youth development are increasingly familiar with this definition, teachers of adolescents are likely to hold their own theories about what 'purpose in life' is, and whether and how it can be supported in secondary classrooms. These same teachers are often taught that it is important to discover what their students already know in order to help them move to higher levels of thinking on any given topic. More specifically, they are taught that part of good teaching involves understanding the existing theories that individuals hold so that evidence can be presented that helps address the specific ways in which those theories may be inadequate or incomplete, while retaining what is accurate and useful (Bransford, Brown, and Cocking 2000). Researchers and practitioners in the field of teacher education also know that, at least in some areas, teacher beliefs influence their practices (Fang 1997), and in many teacher preparation programmes, teachers are envisioned as both reflective practitioners and learners (Adler 1991; Leitch and Day 2000). However, in the evolving effort to understand how to leverage the academic efforts of schools to support purpose in life in students, minimal information exists that highlights teachers' actual beliefs about purpose in life. Given the pedagogical importance for teacher educators of understanding what teachers already believe about purpose in life, the study described here was designed to generate information about purpose in life beliefs among secondary school teachers from a variety of academic disciplines in the United States.

A multidimensional definition of purpose in life offers a heuristic for examining teacher beliefs about the topic. As researchers have worked to identify purpose in adolescents, four underlying dimensions have been proposed: intention, personal meaning, beyond-the-self contribution and engagement (Damon, Menon, and Bronk 2003; Malin et al. 2014; Moran 2009; Yeager and Bundick 2009). These dimensions may be useful starting points for talking with teachers about supporting purpose in their classrooms because they each offer access to a complex construct. In other words, while it may be true that relatively few teachers explicitly design their classroom efforts to support the developmental goal of 'purpose' or utilise a 'purpose' curriculum, it may also be true that many teachers already think about their content area and the futures of their students in ways that align with the individual dimensions of purpose. With this potentiality in mind, the study described here utilised two of the dimensions of purpose, personal meaning and beyond-the-self consequences, in order to unearth secondary school teachers' beliefs about their roles in supporting purpose in life in adolescents.

Why teach for adolescent purpose during the secondary school years?

Specific characteristics of the period of adolescence suggest that working to understand one's purpose in life may be salient to this developmental stage. The prototypical adolescent is engaged in identity exploration (Lerner 2008), and this period of identity exploration lasts until, at least, emerging adulthood (Kroger, Martinussen, and Marcia 2010). Purpose in life may be seen as an expression of identity commitments: 'This is who I am, and therefore this is what I will do in the world'. Unsurprisingly then, research about purpose development also shows a pattern of exploration prior to commitment. For example, during the secondary school years, adolescents do not, on average, find and commit to purpose (Malin et al. 2014). However, Malin et al. (2014) also show that adolescents find personal meaning in their pursuits, set goals for themselves or find an intention, think about ways to contribute to the world and find ways to engage in a variety of pursuits. It is not so much that adolescents are not on the path to purpose, but that, in developmentally appropriate ways, they are not quite there. With the exploratory, uncommitted nature of adolescence in mind, it may be most appropriate for teachers to think about developing purposeful mindsets during adolescence, with an eye to larger and more long-term intentions. If this is done, then the adolescent or young adult who eventually finds a personally meaningful intention to pursue

EDUCATION FOR PURPOSEFUL TEACHING AROUND THE WORLD

has also developed resources to aid in this pursuit by practising goal setting, engagement and beyond-the-self thinking in a variety of areas.

Secondary school teachers may also be interested in learning how to support the development of purpose in life in their students because it is good for their students and may benefit students in the academic areas towards which teachers in schools typically target their work. Research showing that purpose in life is a desired developmental outcome for adolescents, in particular, continues to grow. For example, several correlations have been established between purpose and aspects of adolescent thriving and identity development (Bronk 2011; Bundick et al. 2010; Burrow and Hill 2011; Bronk et al. 2009). Additionally, teachers may be particularly interested in emerging work demonstrating links between both the beyond-the-self and personal meaning dimensions of purpose and academically relevant outcomes. For example, when students are provided with a beyond-the-self reason to work on a task, they stick to challenging, yet not particularly interesting, tasks for longer (Yeager et al. 2014). Related to the purpose dimension of personal meaning, Hulleman and Harackiewicz (2009) showed that low-performing ninth-grade students were more interested in what they were learning and earned higher grades in that subject when they completed written reflections about the personal relevance of what they were studying. Taken together, this research suggests purpose is a good thing to develop in adolescents, but it does not highlight the ways in which purpose may be intentionally fostered.

How may adolescent purpose be supported during the secondary school years?

Research focusing on the specific ways in which purpose may be fostered during adolescence is still relatively nascent, and that which does exist does not highlight specific classroom strategies that would be of particular interest to teachers. Koshy and Mariano (2011) reviewed literature concerning existing programmes designed to support purpose. Finding few contemporary examples, especially in schools, they also described related efforts where these efforts aligned with purpose. For example, they focused on the ways in which schools may support purpose development through civic engagement and service learning. Other researchers have listened to adolescents in order to understand the social supports adolescents identify as they describe their purposes in life. (Moran et al. 2013). Among those identified social supports, adolescents name their schools as one among many contexts in which purpose develops (Moran et al. 2013). Within the school context, student perceptions of teacher competencies have been shown to predict aspects of purpose development (Bundick and Tirri 2014). Overall, however, research that uncovers specific strategies to support purpose is needed (Hill, Burrow, and Sumner 2013).

From a teacher education perspective, two areas of thought from European and American traditions may be especially helpful in considering teacher beliefs about supporting purpose in their adolescent students: Hopmann's (2007) interpretation of 'matter and meaning' as presented in his discussion of *didaktik* and Shulman's (1986) concept of pedagogical content knowledge. *Didaktik,* in German and other European discussions of teacher education, refers to various processes at work in the interaction among teachers, learners and content (Hopmann 2007). The term has no simple English language translation (Hopmann 2007), and a full explication of its meaning is beyond the scope of the study at hand. However, Hopmann (2007) argues that one of the core characteristics of teaching within *didaktik* is the difference between 'matter' and 'meaning'. Matter is the more concrete of the two, refer-ring to the content of teaching (eg US History, Algebra or Art). Meaning, however, refers to deeper truths about humankind and its existence that emerge in the interactions among the learner, teacher and academic content. One of the assumptions of the present study is that purpose in life may be discovered through the individual's interactions with any number of academic disciplines; Hopmann's (2007) language of matter and meaning provides a helpful framework within which to consider these possibilities.

Within the context of teacher education in the United States, the past three decades have seen an increased emphasis on the particular type of knowledge that teachers must have in order to teach effectively. Pedagogical content knowledge brings together what teachers know about the subject matter with what they know about teaching (Shulman 1986). Pedagogical content knowledge includes the topics or components of the subject matter and how to make it comprehensible to students. This point of intersection creates one unique type of teacher knowledge, but if pedagogical content knowledge in the academic content areas is put into conversation with pedagogical content knowledge about purpose, then the type of knowledge a teacher may need is even more specialised. The overarching goal of the present study was to begin to unearth this specialised knowledge about teaching for purpose within the academic disciplines. Shulman is clear to point out that some of this information derives from research, but that it also comes from the 'wisdom of practice' (Shulman 1986, 9). In the effort to understand how to support purpose development through teaching in the academic disciplines, and in turn help teachers learn how to do so, teacher wisdom is a key component of building up the repertoire of pedagogical content knowledge for the subject matter of *purpose*.

Using a dimensional definition of purpose to explore teacher beliefs

The dimensional understanding of purpose introduced earlier offers four different paths for unearthing teacher wisdom about how to teach for purpose. The dimensions of purpose provide the conceptual framework for the methods of the study described here, and may be understood as building blocks or precursors to purpose in life (Malin et al. 2014). For example, one individual may identify the intention of their purpose prior to becoming highly engaged. Another individual may become highly engaged in several activities that positively influence others in some way, and through these activities discover the one thing he or she most intends to accomplish through their life purpose. In the following section, each dimen-sion is described in further detail in order to lay a foundation for using two of these dimen-sions as entry points for investigating teacher beliefs about purpose.

Intention
The intention of one's purpose is a key dimension of the definition of purpose utilised in the present work. This dimension may be understood as the 'content' of purpose, and this par-ticular dimension distinguishes contemporary research about purpose from earlier waves of such research. The earliest research about purpose focused on 'sense of purpose' (Crumbaugh and Maholick 1964). Sense of purpose refers to the feeling or belief that one's life has purpose, and not necessarily the intention of that purpose. In other words, one can believe that one's life has purpose, but not yet know what that purpose is. However, in more contemporary investigations of purpose, researchers have focused on the degree to which

adolescents not only have a sense of purpose, but have also come to understand what that purpose is: they know what they intend to do through their life's purpose.

Personal meaning
Beyond identifying the intention of purpose, the definition of purpose utilised here requires that this intention be personally meaningful to the individual. One can imagine individuals whose multiple goals in life are organised around a larger intention, but who find no meaning in this particular intention, they are simply moving through life. The *personal meaning* dimension of purpose gives credence to the intrinsic value that the individual may find in his or her purpose. Purposeful individuals pursue their purposes, in part, because it brings them joy and satisfaction, or it fulfils intellectual curiosity, among many other potential intrinsic motivators. Imagine a young man who declares that he is going to travel to less developed countries working on water delivery to rural villages. 'Wow!' those around this young man might think, '*This* is a young person with purpose'. However, in further conversation with that young man, the listener hears much more about his love of music, and how much he regrets that he will have to give up this passion of his life in order to work towards his intention of delivering water to rural villages. At this point, working with the understanding of purpose proposed here, there would be several more questions to ask this young man in order to determine whether or not he is truly purposeful. This is because it would seem that he is giving up that which is most personally meaningful to him (music) to pursue something that others are likely to find important (water delivery to rural villages). The dimension of personal meaning honours the ways in which that which is most personally meaningful becomes the path to beyond-the-self contribution, rather than its obstacle.

Beyond-the-self contribution
Purpose also requires that the individual influence the world beyond the self through working to accomplish their intention. As other researchers have noted, intentions to influence the world beyond the self may be prosocial, antisocial or neutral (Damon, Menon, and Bronk 2003), and sorting beyond-the-self intentions into these categories is a task that is somewhat dependent on the values of a particular group about what is good for others and what is not, and about what is the 'self' and what is 'other'. However, purpose also fits in a developmental systems model of adolescent thriving (Bundick et al. 2010). In this model, positive forms of contribution are theorised to be good for both the individual and society (Lerner, Dowling, and Anderson 2003). From this perspective then, assets of the system do not simply orient towards what benefits the individual; these assets also result in the good of the system. The beyond-the-self dimension of purpose, when it is construed as part of this system, is necessarily about positive contribution. Building from this theory, the present work relies on a particular operationalisation of the beyond-the-self dimension of purpose. The beyond-the-self dimension of purpose is met when the individual intends to increase the well-being of family, community or greater society in some way, while refraining from gravely and recklessly harming others in this pursuit.

Engagement
The fourth dimension of purpose is *engagement*. In earlier research on the forms of purpose, researchers noted that while adolescents may articulate a long-term intention that is both personally meaningful and positively contributes to the world in some way, they vary in the

degree to which they take consistent action to work towards these articulated purposes (Malin et al. 2014). In other words, the purposeful individual organises actions around several related goals (McKnight and Kashdan 2009), and thus part of determining if an individual is purposeful is recognising the steps enacted to achieve these related goals.

Engagement with one's purpose may look different at different ages and as one's work towards the intention progresses. For example, an early adolescent girl may describe her purpose in life as helping animals. She may want to do this by becoming a veterinarian, which is something that she knows requires more than four years of college. Clearly, the early adolescent is not enacting her purpose by practising as a 13-year-old veterinarian, but she may volunteer at an animal shelter, and work hard in her classes so that she can gain admission to the types of university programmes that will allow her to go to veterinary school. Through these actions that will help her accomplish that which is most important to her, she demonstrates the dimension of engagement.

Utilising the dimensions of purpose to explore teachers' educational purposes

The primary aim of the study described here was to highlight teacher beliefs about purpose. The dimensions of purpose offer four distinct windows of opportunity for recognising these beliefs. However, two of the dimensions may be particularly important to consider. In a study of 270 adolescents and emerging adults, 42% of college students were purposeful, while another 42% demonstrated self-oriented life goals (all dimensions of purpose except beyond-the-self contribution) (Moran 2009). This finding would suggest that while most individuals find and engage in work to accomplish a long-term intention that is personally meaningful by the time of emerging adulthood, fewer than half incorporate a beyond-the-self compo-nent into these efforts. Therefore, it makes theoretical and practical sense to target teacher beliefs around the integration of that which is personally meaningful with that which is consequential to the world beyond the self because there is at least some evidence that the integration of these two dimensions may benefit from more explicit support, while individ-uals may more typically receive the supports they need to find an intention and engage with it. With this in mind, the present study utilised the individual dimensions of personal meaning and beyond-the-self consequences in order to explore teacher beliefs about purpose, which integrates the two.

Furthermore, this study rests on an assumption that while teachers may or may not directly think about or target the unified construct of purpose through their classroom practices, it is likely that they think about or target at least one or more of its constitutive dimensions in their work. In other words, the ways in which teachers view their educational purposes may provide insight into how teachers may support purpose development in adolescent students. For example, when Finnish student-teachers were asked to reflect in writing on the 'educational purposefulness' of their own teaching, they wrote about their responsibilities to teach about the subject matter, and also about the importance of rela-tionships with their students (Tirri and Ubani 2013), and a similar study of practising Finnish teachers found that teachers saw themselves as responsible for aspects of students ethical growth (Tirri 2012). While the work of Tirri and colleagues has relied on a general prompt to reflect on educational purposefulness, the present study, in part, relies on specific prompts about the dimensions of purpose, but in the context of teachers' views on educational pur-posefulness, rather than through directly asking about purpose in life. By learning about how teachers think about and intend to support each dimension in their overall understanding of the purpose of education within their content area, progress can be made towards the ultimate goal of understanding how to support purpose in the classroom, and in turn how to support teachers in their efforts to do so. The study described here was designed to generate an exploratory and qualitative account of teacher beliefs about purpose, particularly the integration of that which is personally meaningful with that which positively influences the world beyond the self, with the hope that this account might inform both teacher educators and researchers who seek to understand how better to support purpose development in secondary schools.

Methods

The aim of the qualitative study described here was to explore US secondary school teacher beliefs about purpose. The study was designed to answer the following research questions:

(1) In what ways, if any, do US secondary school teachers' thoughts about their educational purposes align with the 'personal meaning' and 'beyond-the-self' dimensions of the researcher-driven definition of purpose in life?

(2) In what ways, if any, do US secondary school teachers' responses to direct questions about purpose in life align with the 'personal meaning' and 'beyond-the-self' dimensions of the researcher-driven definition of purpose in life?

This work is descriptive and theory generating, and therefore there were no hypotheses. The institutional review board at Texas Christian University approved this study.

Participants

The sample for this study was purposive, specifically targeting teachers who were interested in the topic of purpose. High school teachers from the US state of Texas were recruited for this study through email announcements about the study from the primary investigator. Nine teachers responded to these recruitment emails. Three of the teachers taught in a public magnet school focused on developing globally minded citizens. Another three teachers taught in two different larger, public, comprehensive high schools in the same school district as each other. The final three teachers taught at a secular, private high school in the same geographic area as the larger, public, comprehensive schools.

Teacher participants were diverse in gender and experience in teaching. The public magnet school teachers included one female biology teacher, one male economics teacher and one male mathematics teacher, who had all been teaching for less than five years. The comprehensive public school teachers included one female chemistry teacher, one female mathematics teacher and one male English teacher, who had all been teaching for more than five years. The private school teachers were all male, including one English teacher, one writing teacher and one mathematics teacher. The private school teachers also all had more than five years of teaching experience.

School contexts varied in terms of the degree to which holistic educational goals, like purpose in life, might be supported. At both the magnet school and the private school, teachers were expected to teach with more holistic goals in mind. The magnet school was responsible for teaching to the state academic standards, but did so within a larger educational mission to develop globally minded citizens. Teachers at the private school were not bound to teach to the state academic standards, and instead taught to their own high-level academic standards, but the mission of this school also included the spiritual and moral development of its students. Teachers from the public, comprehensive high schools were the least likely to be explicitly directed to attend to the holistic growth of their students. While the public, comprehensive schools were different from each other, at the level of the school, they were each first held accountable to meeting the state academic standards as measured through standardised tests. While the study reported here does not include a full, qualitative account of each of these school contexts, these differences should be kept in mind, as these contexts provide another layer of influence on the ways in which teachers may envision their roles in teaching for purpose.

Interview procedure

Teachers were interviewed using a semi-structured interview protocol designed to elicit their beliefs about teaching for purpose, particularly around the dimensions of intention, personal meaning, beyond-the-self contribution and engagement (Appendix A). Interviews were conducted at a location mutually agreed upon by the researcher and the participating teacher. The semi-structured format allowed the interviewer to ask common questions across the participants, while also allowing the interviewer the freedom to delve into deeper areas of the conversation if research interests arose more idiosyncratically. Interviews were audio-recorded. The total time for explaining the study, gaining consent and conducting the interview was approximately 1 hour. A professional transcriptionist transcribed each interview, and the analytical stage of this study utilised these transcripts.

Analytical procedure

The analytical procedure was based in deductive content analysis, which may be used to extract meanings and intentions from participants' words (Elo and Kyngäs 2008). Specifically, the existing theoretical categories of personal meaning and beyond-the-self contribution were used to organise participant responses. Thus, 'personal meaning' and 'beyond-the-self consequences' became provisional codes (Dey 1993) tied to participants' responses to questions about their educational purposes and more direct questions about their definitions of purpose in life. Provisional coding is considered useful when the researcher has a predetermined set of categories by which he or she wishes to organise the data (Saldaña 2013), such as the two dimensions of purpose utilised here. The specific questions from the interview protocol considered to reveal educational purposes were those related to what teachers thought was most important to learn in their content area, and those related to their hopes, concerns and visions of future success for their students. Here, 'content area' is used interchangeably with 'academic discipline', and refers to the subject matter taught by the teacher (eg chemistry, writing or economics). Teacher beliefs about the definition of 'purpose in life' were coded from their responses to a question that directly asked what this concept meant to them.

To check reliability of the codes, the primary investigator discussed the coding scheme with a second coder who was blind to the hypotheses of the study, and then the second coder separately coded three transcripts. Table 1 shows coding guidelines, agreement and representative vignettes for the coded categories. Agreement between the second coder and the principal investigator was acceptable at levels greater than 85% (Miles, Huberman, and Saldaña 2014) for the following codes: content as a pathway (personal meaning); teacher goals for students (personal meaning; beyond-the-self contribution); and teacher beliefs about purpose (personal meaning; beyond-the-self contribution). A 70% level of agreement was reached for 'content as a pathway – beyond-the-self contribution', with more instances of the second coder recognising an instance when the principal investigator did not, than instances where the second coder did not agree with the principal investigator's assignment of the code. Overall, the principal investigator was a more conservative coder than the second coder, meaning the second coder was more likely than the principal investigator to identify the dimensions of purpose in participant's words. As the principal investigator was the sole coder for most transcripts, the findings that follow should be interpreted as a more conservative account of teacher beliefs about the personal meaning and beyond-the-self dimensions of purpose in life.

Findings

Findings from this study of nine secondary school teachers in the United States are presented in the following order. First, findings related to teacher beliefs about what is most important for students to learn in their content areas (eg mathematics, science or English) are presented. Then, findings related to the ways in which teachers described their hopes and concerns for their students are discussed. Finally, findings related to teacher definitions of purpose are presented. Overall, teachers interested in talking about purpose with a researcher did think about their educational purposes in ways that aligned with the personal meaning and beyond-the-self dimensions of purpose in life. At the same time, teachers' definitions of purpose inconsistently included either personal meaning or beyond-the-self language, and rarely included both.

The content area as a pathway to personal meaning and beyond-the-self contribution

The interview began with questions about the participant's academic content area. Specifically, participants were prompted to discuss that which they thought was most important for students to learn within their content area. The goal in coding these responses according to the dimensions of purpose was to begin to understand whether or not teachers conceived of their academic content area as a possible path to the integration of personal meaning and beyond-the-self consequences that is foundational to purpose. Responses to these questions showed a mostly shared hope across participants that students find some personal meaning in what they learn in the disciplines, as well as evidence that for some teachers, the content area is a path to beyond-the-self contribution.

The strongest theme that emerged from this analytical round was that teachers wanted students to understand that whatever they were learning in the academic content area was connected or relevant to students' lives in some way. For example, the biology teacher described connecting learning about body systems to students' successes on the football field. The chemistry teacher also focused on the effect of food on the body through the lens of chemistry. The private school English teacher described wanting his students to 'wind up

Table 1. Coding scheme, agreement and qualitative examples of teachers' educational purposes and purpose definitions.

	Personal meaning	Beyond-the-self
Coding guidelines and agreement	*Educational Purposes (Agreement: > 85%):* Teacher discusses beliefs about important learning goals in the content area, or hopes or concerns for students or visions of future student success in terms of students making personal connections, finding relevance/doing relevant work, having/finding passion, happiness, interest, personal meaning or excitement about subject matter	*Educational Purposes (Agreement: > 85% for student-related questions; > 70% for content area questions):* Teacher discusses beliefs about using content beyond the classroom to connect with others, influence others, help others, make changes, serve the community, solve problems (outside of the classroom), etc. Teacher discusses hopes, concerns or visions of future student success that include students connecting with others, influencing others, helping others, making changes in the community, serving the community and solving problems
	Purpose Definition (Agreement: > 85%): Teacher defines purpose to include making personal connections, finding relevance/doing relevant work, having/finding passion, happiness, interest, personal meaning and excitement	*Purpose Definition (Agreement: >85%):* Teacher defines purpose to include connecting with others, influencing others, helping others, making changes in the community, serving the community and solving problems
Teachers' Educational Purposes	*When asked about their content area:* 'I have students come into my classroom and tell me that they don't like biology … so I ask them, 'Do you like to breathe? Do you enjoy being able to see things and run?' and this and that. It becomes very evident to them really quickly how big of a part, you know, of their life biology is'. – Biology Teacher, Magnet School	*When asked about their content area:* 'In order to be a good, well-rounded citizen, there are certain scientific things that everyone needs to at least be versed on – not necessarily have already formed an opinion … but at least have background knowledge'. – Biology Teacher, Magnet School
	'[I hope students learn] that our global economies are interconnected and that there are a lot of different inputs into our economy that kind of affect our lives that we sometimes have control over collectively. Sometimes we have control over them individually, and then we also often have no control over them whatsoever'. – Economics Teacher, Magnet School	'I'd say in the top three it's very important to learn how to locate oneself in culture, context, communities, and to think about one's responsibilities to and opportunities within the communities of which one is a part'. – Writing Teacher, Private School
	When asked about students' futures: '[I] sort of want them to go to college and be successful, but any time they're just like ecstatic to share whatever they're doing, it makes a difference because you know that they at least are doing something now … That means a lot to me that they found something to be happy about in life'. – English Teacher, Public School	*When asked about students' futures:* 'I would say striving and trying to do their best to take the things that they've learned from high school, and hopefully if they've gone to college too and really put those into practice and become thinkers, become just real-life problem solvers in whatever job or whatever situation they find themselves in'. – Math Teacher, Magnet School
	'It almost never has to do with the name of the person's job. It almost never has to do with the city, town, country, continent in or on which the person lives. I think it has to do with what they get excited about, and if they seem to get excited about things that, again, are productive, are outward-looking, are aware of a world around themselves, are self-aware and world-aware'. – Writing Teacher, Private School	'[My] biggest hope is that they develop the skills and empathy – and empathy is actually a skill … that will allow them to leverage the remarkable privilege and opportunities that they have to make things better'. – Writing Teacher, Private School

Teachers' definitions of purpose in life

'[Purpose in] life. Okay. I really love my life right now. My family is fantastic and my marriage is *wonderful* and my job is so great. I love the books I'm reading. But it doesn't mean anything unless it will mean something ten years from now. All of this excitement about the present and future plans and these things, if … You know, it's like ask me in ten years if I've been living with purpose [laughs] at this stage in my life. I don't … I mean who has the answer to that, I guess. But I guess what I am trying to say is that I know that I am where I have to be, and I am content with all the things that are the way they are. I work so hard to make them that way and to keep them that way here at work and at home and with my relationships. It's just a happy equilibrium, and I think that's enough'. – Math Teacher, Public School

'When it comes to purpose, like I said, the best thing, like with my kids and students and then with my brothers, is seeing that they're happy and that they enjoy … You know, they're not miserable; that's for sure'. – English Teacher, Public School

'Purpose in life … I think that that's probably one of the reasons that I teach what I do, is because you see how every little piece of all of these different systems end up playing a part together and how things that you may initially see as so insignificant still have this huge role. I think that that's just so incredibly important for all of them to realise that whether or not their role is something that ends up being something where they make some large sum of money or something where they, you know, are living paycheck to paycheck, that those things aren't as important as the connections that– You know, they could be driving a school bus and they're going to be impacting so many different lives. I think that constantly that's kind of the thing we're looking at … I think it's like 300 musicians, and I'll show them how it sounds when they're all warming up and then the piece of music that they can perform together. It's literally cooler than most musical pieces they've ever seen, and it's just trying to point out how valuable every single piece and instrument is to that whole. I think that with biology, that's just so evident, how cool it is that there's all of these different pieces being connected. So I hope that that's something that they always remember, that whether their purpose is something that they see as huge or small, that it's still a purpose and it's still part of the whole'. – Biology Teacher, Magnet School

Table 2. Alignment of teacher beliefs with dimensions of purpose.

	Educational purposes				Definitions of purpose in life	
	Content area		Hopes, concerns, and visions of student success			
	Personal meaning	Beyond-the-self	Personal meaning	Beyond-the-self	Personal meaning	Beyond-the-self
Magnet school						
Biology teacher	•	•	•	•		•
Economics teacher	•	•	•			
Math teacher				•		
Public school						
Chemistry teacher	•		•	•		
Math teacher			•		•	
English teacher	•	•	•	•	•	
Private school						
Math teacher			•			•
English teacher	•	•	•	•	•	•
Writing teacher	•	•	•	•		•

having an understanding of themselves as being invited to participate in a conversation that's been going on for a long, long time'. The economics teacher hoped that his students would learn 'that there are a lot of different inputs into our economy that affect our lives'. All in all, six of the nine teachers touched on some aspect of personal meaning or connection for students when they described what they hoped students learned from the discipline (Table 2).

A second theme that emerged from this analytical stage was that some teachers also wanted students to learn about how they might become a part of their communities, or in the language of purpose, to be of consequence to the world beyond the self. The private school English teacher quoted above went on to say that once students had found their own voices, that he hoped they would be able to 'bring their voices to the table in that conversation and to engage in it authentically. And also to make maybe their own contribution to that conversation … 'The biology teacher quoted above was the most explicit in her articulation of beyond-the-self learning goals for students within biology, saying, 'In order to be a good, well-rounded citizen, there are certain scientific things that everyone needs to at least be versed on – not necessarily have already formed an opinion … but at least have background knowledge'. The writing teacher articulated a hope that students 'think about [their] responsibilities to and opportunities within the communities of which [they] are a part'. Overall, five out of the nine teachers specifically mentioned beyond-the-self consequences as a part of their overall learning goals for students in their discipline, and all five of these teachers also mentioned content area goals related to students developing personal meaning (Table 2).

Envisioning students' futures as personally meaningful and connected to others

The second analytical stage of this study was to uncover the ways in which teachers may be thinking about the personal meaning and beyond-the-self dimensions of purpose in life when they describe their concerns, hopes and visions of future success for their students.

EDUCATION FOR PURPOSEFUL TEACHING AROUND THE WORLD

To that end, participants were asked about their biggest concerns and hopes for students and what they would need to see in a student 10 years beyond graduation to feel that the student was 'successful'. These responses were coded for personal meaning and beyond-the-self ideas. Teachers overwhelmingly named personally meaningful goals or beyond-the-self contribution when they described their concerns and hopes for their students, with eight of the nine teachers describing the importance of finding personal meaning, and six of the nine teachers describing the importance of beyond-the-self contribution (Table 2). Five teachers explicitly referenced both (Table 2).

Eight of the nine teachers specifically discussed their concerns, hopes and visions of future success for their students in ways that suggested they cared that their students eventually created personally meaningful lives (Table 2). While teachers did not use the language of personal meaning, they did talk about happiness, passion, contentment and fulfilment. The biology teacher hoped she would see her students in the future 'pursuing anything that they're passionate about'. Her colleague in the economics department wanted students to be 'stimulated' by whatever they were doing. All three public school teachers made reference to student happiness. For example, the chemistry teacher, describing the students that she felt were likely to go on to contribute to society in a variety of ways, added, 'I think I would want to see happiness for them'. The public school mathematics teacher used the words 'fulfilling', 'content' and 'enjoying themselves' to describe her hopes for her students and their lives. The public school English teacher, who taught several students who might not consider going on to college, was open to many different paths in life for his students, but qualified all of these paths with the statement, 'But at least they're happy doing what their doing, and I think that … that means a lot to me – that they've found something in life to be happy about'. All three private school teachers also discussed aspects of personal meaning when describing their concerns, hopes and visions of future success for their students. The English teacher specifically referenced happiness, while his colleague in the mathematics department wanted to see that students found something to do that was 'gratifying' to them. The writing teacher looked for excitement about things that were both self- and other-aware, saying: 'I think it has to do with what they get excited about, and if they seem to get excited about things that, again, are productive, are outward-looking, are aware of a world around themselves, are self-aware and world-aware'. Note, also, that the writing teacher specifically ties personal meaning to beyond-the-self awareness. Taken together, teachers' answers to questions about their concerns, hopes and visions of future success for their students included a strong theme of wanting students to live lives of personal meaning.

Six of the nine teachers also explicitly mentioned concerns, hopes or visions of future student success that pointed to beyond-the-self aspirations for their students (Table 2). Teachers who mentioned beyond-the-self concerns were evenly distributed across the school types. The biology teacher from the magnet school already recognised this beyond-the-self drive in her students, saying:

> I just think they have not only the opportunities to make these big changes [in the world] but they want to … they have a desire to make things happen that I don't know if my generation ever had. It's not only, 'Hey, these are the problems that are out there,' but they have this desire to figure out ways to change them.

Her colleague in the mathematics department framed his beyond-the-self goals for his students in terms of the ways they would put their problem-solving skills to use, wanting them to 'put those [problem-solving skills] into practice and become thinkers, become real life problem solvers in whatever job or whatever situation they find themselves in'. The chemistry teacher framed her beyond-the-self hopes for her students in terms of a concern: 'My biggest concern is that the students a lot of times don't get the message that they are capable of being an important part of society and they should be important contributors to society. That is my biggest concern'. The public school English teacher emphasised the possibility that his students would connect with other people, no matter what path they took. Describing students with an interest in auto mechanics, he said, 'That's what they do, and they find opportunities to share that with other people, whether it's working on side projects or whatever [else]'. Two teachers from the private school emphasised contribution in the way they described their hopes for students as well. The English teacher included beyond-the-self involvement when he discussed what he would need to see 10 years after graduation to know that his students were successful:

> I would need to see that the person had gained some autonomy in his life or her life, that they were kind of out there doing it on their own, that their life was involved with others in one way or another, whether it was just through the establishment of their own families or their outreach to the community at large, and that they were doing something creative and constructive and something that makes them happy.

The writing teacher specifically addressed concerns related to the amount of privilege and power his students possessed and would continue to possess: '[My] biggest hope is that they develop the skills and empathy – and empathy is actually a skill ... that will allow them to leverage the remarkable privilege and opportunities that they have to make things better'. Overall, six out of the nine teachers, two from each of the school types included in this study, mentioned beyond-the-self concerns when they described their concerns, hopes and visions of future success for their students (Table 2).

Teachers' definitions of purpose in life

Towards the end of the interview, the interviewer introduced the term 'purpose in life' to participants without providing a researcher-created definition, and then prompted participants to explain what the term meant to them. Some chose to answer this question by explaining their own purposes, while others described the concept of purpose in life in more abstract terms. In contrast to the ways in which several teachers described their educational purposes to include both personal meaning and beyond-the-self consequences, their definitions of purpose in life were less likely to include these two dimensions. In fact, while three teachers included aspects of personal meaning in their definitions, and four included aspects of a beyond-the-self orientation, only one teacher included both of these in his definition of purpose in life.

Teachers who included aspects of personal meaning in their definitions of purpose in life primarily referred to contentment and happiness. For example, the public school English teacher said, 'When it comes to purpose ... the best thing, like with my kids and students and then with my brothers, is seeing that they're happy and that they enjoy ... You know, they're not miserable; that's for sure'. The English teacher from the private school, in the context of describing a more beyond-the-self aspect of purpose, included this qualifier: ' ... but also that by participating in [the beyond-the-self activity] as fully as possible, it's going to enrich me and enrich my experience here'. The mathematics teacher from the public school, who referred to her own purpose in life in order to describe the concept, described finding a 'happy equilibrium'. Overall, three of the nine teachers included aspects of personal meaning in their discussion of purpose in life (Table 2).

Teachers who included aspects of beyond-the-self contribution in their discussions of purpose primarily focused on the idea of recognising and living out one's role in a community or group of people. Two teachers from the private school described purpose in this way. The English teacher explained that purpose means recognising that 'It's important to acknowledge and to know that there's something in this world more than just me that I'm connected with'. His colleague in the maths department described purpose as including 'making contributions to a group and doing so through leadership of that group'. He went on to say:

> That group can be the varsity [American] football team, a very well defined collection of 25 young men, or the president of the student body, a very well defined group of 400 students. But the group can also be kids who hang out in this room typically [during] fourth period. There's no formal election of gathering … But at any rate, to help a group achieve laudable goals. Your group could be Firestone, a tire store, and obviously part of that purpose is to realize a profit. But hopefully you're also, having a purpose of ethical service to the customer … But I would say a general purpose for people would be to see themselves in a variety of groups, and see how they can help that group.

The biology teacher from the magnet school also stressed the importance of recognising one's interconnectedness as being central to purpose. She connected this theme to her content area as well, and stated:

> I think that that's probably one of the reasons that I teach what I do, is because you see how every little piece of all of these different systems end up playing a part together and how things that you may initially see as so insignificant still have this huge role (see Table 1 for a more extended version of this quote).

Overall, four teachers included aspects of beyond-the-self contribution in the way that they described purpose in life (Table 2).

Summary of results

The study described here was designed to understand the degree to which teachers' educational purposes and definitions of purpose in life align with the personal meaning and beyond-the-self dimensions of the researcher-driven definition of purpose. Teachers were interviewed about their beliefs about their academic content areas, their hopes, concerns and visions of future success for their students and about their own definitions of purpose in life. Their responses revealed that several of the teachers conceived of their educational purposes in ways that aligned with the personal meaning and beyond-the-self dimensions of purpose. However, when directly prompted to discuss the concept of purpose in life, this alignment was less clear.

Discussion

The aim of the study described here was to create an account of what teachers already believe about supporting purpose in their classrooms, with the ultimate goal of providing points of departure for future research and for teacher professional development opportunities targeted towards teaching for purpose. This aim was grounded in what is known about how individuals learn and in what is known about what teachers need to know to teach well. Specifically, a key part of helping individuals develop more productive theories in any given area is to understand the existing theories that they hold (Bransford, Brown, and Cocking 2000). Additionally, one of the types of knowledge that teachers need to teach well is pedagogical content knowledge, which can, in part, be gathered from the wisdom of practice (Shulman 1986). Teachers' beliefs about their educational purposes offer researchers a way to learn about how teachers may support the development of purpose in their students (Tirri 2012; Tirri and Ubani 2013). The findings of this study suggest that teachers who are interested in talking about purpose already think in deep ways about how their content area provides a pathway to finding personal meaning and considering beyond-the-self consequences, and that their concerns, hopes and visions of future success for their students also align with these two dimensions of purpose. When directly prompted, however, their own definitions of purpose were less likely to include personal meaning and beyond-the-self consequences. Possible interpretations for these findings are discussed here, and implications for future research and work with teachers are addressed.

'Matter and meaning' in the content area

While this study listened to the voices of American teachers who likely did not experience teacher training immersed in *didaktik* as articulated by Hopmann (2007), their words suggest that US teachers interested in talking about purpose are also somewhat likely to believe their content area (the 'matter' of their teaching) is a pathway to 'meaning', specifically the personal meaning and beyond-the-self dimensions of purpose in life. Six of the nine teachers in this study saw their content area as a pathway to at least one of these two dimensions, and five included both dimensions as they discussed what was most important to learn in the content area. This is, perhaps, not surprising, as teachers may teach what they themselves find meaningful or useful.

The fact that teachers hoped students would find personal meaning and ways to act beyond the self through their learning in academic content areas is particularly salient when the identity exploratory nature of adolescence is considered (Kroger, Martinussen, and Marcia 2010). Inherent in the definition of purpose utilised in this study is that individuals move from having a general sense of purpose to knowing what that purpose is. The content of one's purpose (the intention) is then key, according to this definition, to having purpose. Teachers who teach in their content areas with an eye towards how what is learned in the content area may be both personally meaningful and influence the world beyond the self are exposing students to a variety of possible intentions.

The fact that several teachers in this study discussed their academic content in ways that align with the personal meaning and beyond-the-self dimensions of purpose has implications for how teachers are introduced to and supported in their efforts to teach for purpose. A potential objection to teaching for purpose might be that there is simply not enough time in the standards- and assessment-driven environment in many US schools, and in the schools of many other nations. Educators may view purpose education as simply 'one more thing' for which there is no time. However, the teachers in this study show that helping teachers teach for purpose may be more about helping them tap into the greater meaning they find in the particular subject matter they teach, rather than giving teachers a whole new subject (purpose) to include in their teaching. Teacher educators who wish to support teachers in their efforts to teach for purpose then may want to begin with having these individuals explore what they already believe is the most important thing for students to learn in the content area, and then layer a discussion about purpose on top of this existing teacher knowledge.

Teachers want purposeful futures for their students

When asked to describe their hopes, concerns and visions of future success for their students, teachers also spoke in ways that aligned with the personal meaning and beyond-the-self dimensions of purpose in life. As with the ways in which they spoke about their content areas, most teachers expressed hopes that their students would create personally meaningful lives that reached beyond the self in some way, with slightly more than half of the participating teachers integrating personal meaning and beyond-the-self consequences in their responses to these questions.

This finding helps address another concern that teachers may have about teaching for purpose. Some teachers may feel that teaching for purpose in life is a large task beyond the scope of the academic responsibilities of schools. However, as with teacher beliefs about their content areas, teachers' expressions of their concerns, hopes and visions of future success for students offer another path to helping teachers think about how they might support purpose in their classrooms. While it may feel like an overwhelmingly large responsibility for a teacher to consider shaping purpose in life, it may feel more approachable for a teacher to think about helping a student find something that is personally meaningful, or introducing a student to way to contribute to the world beyond the self. As with using content area goals as an entry point, teacher educators who want to support teachers in their efforts to develop purpose in their students may want to consider beginning the discussion with a discussion of the goals that teachers already hold for their students, followed by learning activities that show how some of those existing goals align with the dimensions of purpose.

Teachers' definitions of purpose

When teachers were asked to provide their own definitions of purpose in life, they did not consistently provide definitions that addressed the personal meaning and beyond-the-self dimensions of purpose, with less than half of the group including each of these, and only one participant including both. Beginning with the language of 'purpose' did not surface teacher thinking about the integration of personal meaning with beyond-the-self consequences in the way that allowing teachers to talk about their educational purposes did. When the dimensions were used as a starting point, teacher beliefs about the dimensions of purpose were plentiful, but when specifically prompted to discuss purpose, the same complexity did not emerge.

This finding, too, has implications for professional development efforts that aim to support secondary teachers as they support purpose in life in their students. Beginning professional development efforts without first offering opportunities for teachers to come to a multidimensional understanding of purpose through reflecting on their own educational purposes may prematurely cut short teacher thinking in this area. A teacher may be inclined to think, 'This is what purpose is, and I do not teach about that'. Instead, it may be worthwhile to encourage teachers to reflect on the ways in which they support students in creating personal meaning or in thinking in beyond-the-self ways about what they are learning, without yet naming these as 'purpose'. Then, drawing from the meaning that teachers likely already think is created through the teaching and learning process in their academic content areas, teacher educators may facilitate a process by which the multidimensional definition of purpose is co-constructed from what teachers already think and do, as these thoughts and practices are put into conversation with the researcher-driven definition.

Implications for teacher education and professional development

This investigation of teacher beliefs about purpose began with an argument based in learning theory (that in order to teach a student well; to change their existing theories about anything): the teacher must have a strong understanding of the student's existing knowledge or theories about the subject (Bransford, Brown, and Cocking 2000). When thinking about how to best educate future and current teachers to teach for purpose, the teachers are the students whose existing theories teacher educators must understand. A key finding of the study described here is that when teachers are directly asked to discuss their understanding of 'purpose', they do so in ways that are less likely to integrate personal meaning and beyond-the-self consequences than when those same teachers are asked to reflect on their educational purposes in a variety of ways. In this case, teachers' existing theories about their educational purposes may provide a clearer pathway than their theories about the unified construct of purpose for helping them consider how they might teach for purpose. In much the way that Hulleman and Harackiewicz (2009) demonstrated that high school students performed better when they were able to reflect on the ways in which what they were learning was relevant to them, teacher educators may find it beneficial to begin their professional development efforts with learning activities that encourage future and current teachers to reflect on the ways in which personal meaning and beyond-the-self consequences are relevant to what they teach (the content area) and their goals for who they teach (their hopes, concerns and visions of future success for their students). This may be especially beneficial for future and current teachers who will teach in contexts that do not explicitly include holistic learning goals for students, and for whom the relevance of teaching for purpose may be less immediately clear.

Put another way, the findings of this study suggest that teacher educators may find it helpful to create learning opportunities that encourage future and current teachers to consider the 'meaning' that is created between student, teacher and subject matter (Hopmann 2007). The academic disciplines represented in this study were diverse, and not a single participant answered questions with only simple, concrete references to the subject matter. All nine participants articulated at least some ways in which they hoped students learned about deeper truths in life from their encounters with the specific subject matter of their classrooms. Tirri and Ubani's (2013) work offers a path forward from this finding; perhaps teacher educators can consider asking future teachers to reflect on their own educational purposes so that 'meaning' stays more in the forefront of teacher thinking as they begin their daily teaching practice. Yeager and Walton (2011) have explained how brief interventions in educational settings, such as reflective writing, set into motion recursive processes that have more long-term impact. It may be that brief reflective activities during teacher preparation would set into motion more long-term thinking about how to help students integrate personal meaning and beyond-the-self contribution through the lessons of various academic content areas. Awareness of the range of possible meanings that may be created through teacher and student interactions with each other and the subject matter, may, in fact, be the pedagogical content knowledge (Shulman 1986) that teachers need to teach effectively for purpose. Likewise, those who facilitate professional development opportunities for practising teachers may also want to consider offering these spaces for reflection on the ways in which meaning is created across a variety of academic disciplines.

Implications for future research

The implications of this exploratory work for future research align with implications for teacher education and professional development. Specifically, in the effort to understand how purpose is and may be supported in secondary classrooms, researchers may want to consider structuring their investigations around the individual dimensions, rather than the integrated construct of purpose. Particularly in the evolving effort to understand *practices* to support purpose, looking through the lens of the dimensions may unearth several practices that would be missed through the lens of the integrated construct. Another implication of these findings for researchers is that practising teachers who are interested in the topic of purpose are valuable sources of information and potential collaborative partners in continued efforts to generate evidence-based practices for supporting purpose in the classroom. Future research efforts will likely benefit from working with teachers to create and understand the practices of purposeful classrooms, rather than simply delivering research findings and curriculum about purpose to teachers.

Limitations

While the findings of this study offer hope that purpose can be supported in the classroom, and that there are teachers doing this work and interested in learning more about it, there are limitations that future studies in this area should address. A key limitation is the small sample size. Nine teachers provided a wealth of information about what is possible when researchers seek out teacher expertise, but the field would benefit from future work that samples larger numbers of teachers from diverse content areas and school settings. Additionally, future work in this area should complement the interview method utilised in this study with student data that would help offer stronger support that students experience learning across the dimensions of purpose in the ways that their teachers hope they do.

Conclusion

This exploratory study of secondary teachers' beliefs about the personal meaning and beyond-the-self dimensions of purpose was grounded in the belief that teachers are learners and experts to whom researchers should turn in order to better understand how to support purpose in adolescent students. As they shared from the wisdom of their practice, the teachers in this study did not disappoint, each providing rich and varied information about the ways in which they think about their academic content area and their concerns, hopes and visions of future success for students. In many ways, their thoughts about these aspects of their educational purposes aligned with the personal meaning and beyond-the-self dimensions of purpose. Those who work to educate future and current teachers may be able to leverage what teachers think about their educational purposes to help teachers support purpose development in adolescent students. Continuing to include teachers as key partners

Disclosure statement

No potential conflict of interest was reported by the author.

Funding

This research was supported by the Donovan and Patton College of Education Impact Grant at Texas Christian University, the Texas Christian University Junior Faculty Summer Research Program, and the Texas Christian University Research and Creative Activities Fund.

References

Adler, S 1991. "The Reflective Practitioner and the Curriculum of Teacher-education." *Journal of Education for Teaching* 17 (2): 139–150.

Bransford, J. D., A. L. Brown, and R. R. Cocking. 2000. *How People Learn: Brain, Mind, Experience, and School (Expanded Edition)*. Washington, DC: National Academy Press.

Bronk, K. C. 2011. "The Role of Purpose in Life in Healthy Identity Formation: A Grounded Model." *New Directions for Youth Development* 2011 (132): 31–44. doi:10.1002/yd.426.

Bronk, K., P. L. Hill, D. K. Lapsley, T. L. Talib, and H. Finch. 2009. "Purpose, Hope, and Life Satisfaction in Three Age Groups." *The Journal of Positive Psychology* 4 (6): 500–510. doi:10.1080/17439760903271439.

Bundick, M. J., and K. Tirri. 2014. "Student Perceptions of Teacher Support and Competencies for Fostering Youth Purpose and Positive Youth Development: Perspectives from Two Countries." *Applied Developmental Science* 18 (3): 148–162. doi:10.1080/10888691.2014.924357.

Bundick, M. J., D. S. Yeager, P. E. King, and W. Damon. 2010. "Thriving across the Life Span." In *The Handbook of Life-span Development*, edited by R. M. Lerner, M. E. Lamb, and A. M. Freund, 882–923. New York: Wiley.

Burrow, A. L., and P. L. Hill. 2011. "Purpose as a Form of Identity Capital for Positive Youth Adjustment." *Developmental Psychology* 47 (4): 1196–1206. doi:10.1037/a00023818.

Crumbaugh, J. C., and L. T. Maholick. 1964. "An Experimental Study in Existentialism: The Psychometric Approach to Frankl's Concept of Noogenic Neurosis." *Journal of Clinical Psychology* 20 (2): 200–207.

Damon, W., J. Menon, and K. Bronk. 2003. "The Development of Purpose during Adolescence." *Applied Developmental Science* 7 (3): 119–128. doi:10.1207/S1532480XADS0703_2.

Dey, I. 1993. *Qualitative Data Analysis: A User-friendly Guide for Social Scientists*. New York: Routledge.

Elo, S., and H. Kyngäs. 2008. "The Qualitative Content Analysis Process." *Journal of Advanced Nursing* 62 (1): 107–115.

Fang, Z. 1997. "A Review of Research on Teacher Beliefs and Practices." *Educational Research* 38 (1): 47–65.

Hill, P. L., A. L. Burrow, and R. Sumner. 2013. "Addressing Important Questions in the Field of Adolescent Purpose." *Child Development Perspectives* 7 (4): 232–236. doi:10.1111/cdep.12048.

Hopmann, S. 2007. "Restrained Teaching: The Common Core of Didaktik." *European Educational Research Journal* 6 (2): 109–124.

Hulleman, C. S., and J. M. Harackiewicz. 2009. "Promoting Interest and Performance in High School Science Classes." *Science* 326 (5958): 1410–1412. doi:10.1126/science.1177067.

Koshy, S. I., and J. Mariano. 2011. "Promoting Youth Purpose: A Review of the Literature." *New Directions for Youth Development* 2011 (132): 13–29. doi:10.1002/yd.425.

Kroger, J., M. Martinussen, and J. E. Marcia. 2010. "Identity Status Change during Adolescence and Young Adulthood: A Meta-analysis." *Journal of Adolescence* 33 (5): 683–698. doi:10.1016/j.adolescence.2009.11.002.

Leitch, R., and C. Day. 2000. "Action Research and Reflective Practice: Towards a Holistic View." *Educational Action Research* 8 (1): 179–193. doi:10.1080/09650790000200108.

EDUCATION FOR PURPOSEFUL TEACHING AROUND THE WORLD

Lerner, R. 2008. "Spirituality, Positive Purpose, Wisdom, and Positive Development in Adolescence: Comments on Oman, Flinders, and Thorensen's Ideas about 'Integrating Spiritual Modeling into Education.'" *The International Journal for the Psychology of Religion* 18 (2): 108–118. doi:10.1080/10508610701879340.

Lerner, R. M., E. M. Dowling, and P. A. Anderson. 2003. "Positive Youth Development: Thriving as the Basis of Personhood and Civil Society." *Applied Developmental Science* 7 (3): 172–180. doi:10.1002/yd.14.

Malin, H., T. S. Reilly, B. Quinn, and S. Moran. 2014. "Adolescent Purpose Development: Exploring Empathy, Discovering Roles, Shifting Priorities, and Creating Pathways." *Journal of Research on Adolescence* 24 (1): 186–199. doi:10.1111/jora.12051.

McKnight, P. E., and T. B. Kashdan. 2009. "Purpose in Life as a System That Creates and Sustains Health and Well-being: An Integrative, Testable Theory." *Review of General Psychology* 13 (3): 242–251.

Miles, M. B., A. M. Huberman, and J. Saldaña. 2014. *Qualitative Data Analysis: A Methods Sourcebook.* 3rd ed. Thousand Oaks, CA: Sage.

Moran, S. 2009. "Purpose: Giftedness in Intrapersonal Intelligence." *High Ability Studies* 20 (2): 143–159. doi:10.1080/13598130903358501.

Moran, S., M. J. Bundick, H. Malin, and T. S. Reilly. 2013. "How Supportive of Their Specific Purposes Do Youth Believe Their Family and Friends Are?" *Journal of Adolescent Research* 28 (3): 348–377. doi:10.1177/0743558412457816.

Saldaña, J. 2013. *The Coding Manual for Qualitative Researchers.* 2nd ed. Thousand Oaks, CA: Sage.

Shulman, L. 1986. "Those Who Understand: Knowledge Growth in Teaching." *Educational Researcher* 15 (2): 4–14.

Tirri, K. 2012. "The Core of School Pedagogy: Finnish Teachers' Views of the Educational Purposefulness of Their Teaching." In *Miracle of Education,* edited by H. Niemi, A. Toom, and A. Kallioniemi, 55–66. Rotterdam: Sense Publishers.

Tirri, K., and M. Ubani. 2013. "Education of Finnish Student Teachers for Purposeful Teaching." *Journal of Education for Teaching* 39 (1): 21–29. doi:10.1080/02607476.2012.733188.

Yeager, D. S., and M. J. Bundick. 2009. "The Role of Purposeful Work Goals in Promoting Meaning in Life and in Schoolwork during Adolescence." *Journal of Adolescent Research* 24 (4): 423–452. doi:10.1177/0743558409336749.

Yeager, D. S., M. Henderson, D. Paunesku, G. M. Walton, S. D'Mello, B. J. Spitzer, and A. L. Duckworth. 2014. "Boring but Important: A Self-transcendent Purpose for Learning Fosters Academic Self-regulation." *Journal of Personality and Social Psychology* 107 (4): 559–580. doi:10.1037/a0037637.

Yeager, D. S., and G. M. Walton. 2011. "Social-psychological Interventions in Education: They're Not Magic." *Review of Educational Research* 81 (2): 267–301. doi:10.3102/0034654311405999.

Appendix A. Semi-structured teacher interview protocol

Introduction	• Tell me a little bit about yourself.
	• Tell me a little bit about why you became a teacher.
Elicit purpose for content area	• (If not already answered) Tell me a little bit about the main content area you teach.
	• Why do you teach in this content area?
	• What do you think is most important for students to learn in this content area?
Elicit purpose in general	• What are your biggest concerns for your students?
	• What are your biggest hopes for your students?
	• If you encountered one of your students 10 years after he or she graduated from high school, what would make you think he or she had become successful?
Elicit connections between purpose for content and purpose in general	• Can you talk to me a little about how, if at all, what students learn in your classroom is connected to the things you would like to see in them after they have graduated from high school?
Elicit purpose practices across four dimensions	I would like to spend some time talking about some of the things you do in your classroom to help students learn what is most important in your content

(Continued)

EDUCATION FOR PURPOSEFUL TEACHING AROUND THE WORLD

Appendix 1. (*Continued*).

Goal identification/intention	• Some teachers believe it makes sense for teachers to set the goals of a classroom, and others believe it makes sense for students to set these goals. Can you talk to me about your own thoughts about this? • Was there ever a time when a student of yours developed a personal goal about something related to your content area that he or she wanted to accomplish? Can you tell me about this? • What are some of the things you do to help students set goals like these?
Personal meaning	• Sometimes, students seem to find personal meaning in something they are being taught, and other times, it seems really difficult for them to make that personal connection. Do you think it's important for students to find personal meaning in what they are being taught? • Was there a time in your classroom when you really felt like you sparked those personal connections? Can you tell me about one of these times? • In general, what are some of the things you do in your classroom to try to create personal meaning? • You have mentioned students who have found personal connections with something in your content area. When you see that in a student, what do you do?
Engagement	• What does a student who is engaged with what he or she is learning look like to you? • Have there been times when you felt like your students were really engaged in something you were doing with them? Can you tell me about one of these times? • How do you encourage students to engage or participate in what they are learning in your classes?
Contribution/beyond-the-self	• In most content areas, we can think about knowledge or skills, and then we can think about the ways in which knowledge and skills get used in and beyond the classroom. How do you approach these two ways of thinking about your content area in your own classroom? • (*If above leads to this*) What do you do to help students see how the knowledge and skills of your content area are used beyond the classroom? • Some people say it's important for schools to encourage students to think about how to make their communities and world better, and others think that responsibility mainly belongs to others.• What are your own thoughts about this? • How do you expose your students to some of the ways knowledge and skills from your content area can be used to contribute?
Elicit integrated purpose practices	So far we have discussed things you do in your classroom to encourage your students to identify and set goals, such as … , and what you do to help them find personal meaning and engage in what they do, such as …. We have also discussed how you help students think about how to use what they learn beyond the classroom, such as …. • Are there any ways in which you see that these four things fit together? Lead into one another? • Conceptually? • In your practices? • What are some of the things you do in your classroom that support more than one of these?
Elicit holistic purpose definition and beliefs about teacher roles	Some people believe that everyone has a purpose in life. What does 'purpose in life' mean to you? Some researchers define purpose as being engaged in a life-long intention to accomplish something that is both personally meaningful and contributes to the world in some way. Using this definition, what do you think a teacher's role is in helping students find their purpose in life? • Why? Why not? • What are some of the things you do in your classroom to help students find their purpose in life?
Final check	Throughout the interview, you have talked about a lot of things you do in your classroom, such as …. Do these seem correct? You have also shared your thoughts about how these things relate, such as …. Does this seem correct? Finally, you've talked about (role of teacher in purpose development) …. Does this seem correct? Is there anything else I've missed that you think is important?

Index

Note: **Boldface** page numbers refer to tables and italic page numbers refer to figures.

academic disciplines, purpose within 80
accurate perception 41
active-learning approaches 34
adolescent purpose, in secondary classrooms 83–5; academic disciplines 80; coding scheme, agreement and qualitative examples **86–7**; diverse in gender 83; experience in teaching 83; identity exploration 78; interview procedure 84; pedagogical content knowledge 80; purpose in life 77–9, 90–1; school contexts 83, 84; school teachers 79; social supports 79; teacher beliefs 80–3; teacher education 3, 78–80; *see also* US secondary school teacher
American studies: dabblers group 9, 12; disengaged group in 8, 13; dreamers group 8–9, 12; purposeful teaching group 9; teachers 3
analyses of variance (ANOVAs) 49
Arantes, Valeria Amorim 3
Araujo, Ulisses F. 3

beyond-the-self dimension 32, 81, 85, 91, 92
beyond-the-self hopes 90
beyond-the-self-orientation (BTS) 11, 12
Bildung 8, 21–2
Bransford, J. 2
Brazilian experience in training teachers: cognitive and verbal abilities 32; educational interventions 32; education for purpose 31–3; innovative pedagogies for youth purpose 34–5; pedagogical skills 32; purpose based on values 33–4; teacher training programme 35; water filter for cooking 35–6; website for youth 36
Brazilian Sign Language 35
BTS *see* beyond-the-self-orientation
Bundick, M. 11, 17

Chinese college teachers' competence 4; background and academic achievement 49; college curriculum 41; conception of purpose 43–4; entrance examination 46; life goal ranks 47; major and grade-level students' perceptions 49–50; political education course 45; professional development 41; purpose search, identification and engagement 47, 51; for purpose support 47–9; research practice 52–3; self-evaluations 49; self purpose orientation 50–1; social supports 44; students' purpose support 41, 44–6, 50; students rating 52; teaching experience 45
congruence 4
consequences of one's actions 48
Cotton Bronk, K. 11

Damon, W. 4, 8, 11, 12, 61, 65, 70
Danza, Hanna Cebel 3
Darling-Hammond, L. 2
deaf students, learning periodic table 35
Design Thinking principles 3, 34
didaktik 2, 7, 21, 80, 92
discussing purpose, Finnish and Iranian teachers 17

engagement, purpose and 1, 42, 48, 51, 62, 64, 67, 81–2, 98

Finnish and Iranian teachers 3, 4; *Bildung and Pure Life* 21–2; class and subject **25**, **26**; dimensions 23; discussing purpose 17; educational policies in 19–21, **20**; Ethical Sensitivity Scale Questionnaire 23; guiding purpose in life 24, 25; in-service and pre-service 27; means and standard deviations of **24**; moral profession in 18–19; one-lesson/one-classroom approach 17; pedagogical freedom 21; positive psychology 17; purpose in school environment 16–17, 24–5; regression analysis for 26; self-perceptions 24; teaches future planning 17; youth purpose development 17

INDEX

Finnish teacher education 3, 4; aim for 13; American studies groups 8–9; beyond-the-self-orientation 11, 13; classroom based on 8, 9; empirical findings on 10; ethical values 8; German tradition 7; goal-directedness 11, 13; purpose, concept of 10; of religious education 14; research-based knowledge 8; sense of purpose 11; student teachers' purpose profiles **12**, *13*, *14*; subject-teacher students 8; teaching-studying-learning process 8; young adults 9; *z* -scores, means of *13*
Frankl, V. E. 1, 10

Garbin, Monica 3
Gholami, Khalil 4
goal-directedness 2, 11, 13

Harackiewicz, J. M. 79, 94
Hopmann, S. 8, 92, 94
Hulleman, C. S. 94

identity exploration, adolescent 78
in-service education 20
'intentionality paradox' 58
intention of one's purpose 80–1
Iranian teachers *see* Finnish and Iranian teachers
Islamisation 19

Jiang, Fei 4
John Templeton Foundation 3
Journal of Education for Teaching 1

Kansanen, P. 9
K-means algorithm 12
Koshy, S. 17
Kuusisto, Elina 3–4, 17, 18

life goal ranks, students 47, **50**
life purpose 47, 57, 58, 63, 66
Lin, Shan 4

Mariano, J. M. 4, 11, 17
Moran, S. 3, 4

National Core Curriculum 21
National Core Curriculum for Basic Education (2014) 22

one-lesson/one-classroom approach 17
'one size fits all' curriculum 59

Pahlavi Dynasty 19
pedagogical content knowledge 9, 79, 80, 92, 95
persistence towards accomplishment 48
personal identity 33–4

personal meaning: beyond-the-self contribution and 85–8, **88**, 92, 94–5; dimension of 31, 61, 64, 67, 81, 89, 90, 98
personal purpose 43
Pinheiro, Viviane Potenza Guimarães 3
political education 45, 52
Problem-Based Learning 3, 34–6
Project-Based Learning 3, 34–6
provisional coding 84
Pure Life, in Finland and Iran education 21–2
purpose 43; academic context on 44; based on values 33–4; as career guidance 62–3; Chinese conception of 43–4; content 59; in educational context 2, 3, 58–9; finding place in world 63–5; as form of self-regulation 57; prosocial conceptualisation of 1; teaching 17, 18; as trickle down process 62; *see also* purpose dimensions; youth purpose, teachers on
purpose dimensions 4; beyond-the-self impact 62–4, 67; engagement 1, 42, 48, 51, 62, 64, 67, 81–2, 98; intention 61, 63–5, 67; personal meaning 61, 63, 64–5, 67, 81, 90, 98
purpose education 4, 10, 45, 52, 73, 92; Chinese 42; scientific study of 3; subject matter 4–5
purposeful teaching 2; around the world 3–5

Qajar Dynasty (1794–1925) 19
Quick Cluster Analysis 12
Quinn, B. 3, 4

reflective writing 94
research-based approach 9
research-based knowledge 8
Revised Youth Purpose Survey 47
Roberts, B. W. 11
Robins, R. W. 11
role modelling purposefulness 67
Ryff, C. D. 11

self-concept 33
self-regulation 44, 57, 58, 74
sense of purpose 2, 7, 8, 11, 44, 80–1
social purpose 43, 44
social supports: adolescents 79; schools 44
SPSS 20.0 49
student(s): ethical growth 82; perceptions of teacher competence 49–50, 52; purpose support 3, 41, 44–6, 51, **51**; self-knowledge 32; self purpose orientation 50–1; teachers relationships 82

teacher beliefs, purpose to explore 80; beyond-the-self contribution 81, 83, 91; dimensions of purpose 82–3, **88**; engagement 81–2; intention 80–1; personal meaning 81, 83
TFFTES 22

INDEX

Theoretical Foundation of Fundamental Transformation in the Educational System of the Islamic Republic of Iran 19

Tirri, K. 3, 4, 11, 17, 94

t -tests 49

Ubani, M. 94

Universal Human Rights Declaration 35

University of São Paulo 35

US secondary school teacher 17, 79; analytical procedure 84–5; beliefs about educational purposes 92; beyond-the-self contribution 89–91; education and professional development 94–5; envisioning students' futures 88–90; future research 95; interview procedure 84; matter and meaning 92–3; participants 83–4; personal meaning and beyond-the-self contribution 85–8; purpose education 92; purpose in life 90–1, 93–4

Walton, G. M. 94

Yeager , D. S. 94

youth purpose, teachers on 59; as architect of opportunities 63–5; behavioural pattern 69–70, **70**; beyond-the-self impact 62–4, 67; as coach 65–6; coherent curriculum 71; community context 72; competence 59; current and imagined future efforts 69–70; engagement 62, 64, 67; ideas and actions 60–1, 71; informational pattern 70, **70**; integration of purpose dimensions 72–3; intention 61, 63–5, 67; own purpose development 67–9, **68**, **69**; personal meaning 61, 63, 64–5, 67; practices 60–2; pupil-agentic projects 65–6; qualitative data analyses 61–2, 67; relational pattern 69, **70**; responses 66–7; role-modelling approach 63; sample and data collection 60–1; self-oriented focus 71–2; structure lessons around pupil contributions 73–4; as unchanging 62–3; understandings of life purpose 58